Dearest Lorna
many Blessings
Love
Clairine ♡

I

A therapeutic poetry and meditation guide.

LOTUS LIFTING

Clairine Potter

IV

PREFACE

A journey through the layers of confinement, to find freedom in the words and practices that lifted the lotus to a place of solace and beauty in life.

Forever grateful to PachaMama for the medicine of ayahuasca to surrender one to the knowledge that love, support and guidance has always been with you.

A discovery that we are one and in compassion we grow into the light and love of the Universe and Earth.

A book of seventeen emotional elements to reflect on self-love, acceptance and appreciation.

Lotus Lifting: here's to the journey, to the loved and lost, to all my teachers.

I thank the gods for this here ditty from Source,
and others of course.

To find yourself when you had only been lost,
is a treasure that mustn't be forgot.
So, open up and delve right in,
the uncomfortable is where you begin.

Shed the layers that society has dressed you in.
Dare to be you,
and in this naked form place your garments of love, purity, release,
and surrender into you.

As it's in the moments that we can just be,
where we find our true integrity.
So read the poems,
sit in the still,
because you are divine beauty,
dear lotus, live.

To look into the pages and the space, is where the masterpiece of you can
be unfolded.
Trust your process,
let it go.
The elements of this book will show your truth.

I thank the shamans,
the medicines of Earth,
the loves of loves lost.

Though they won't grow,
So dear lotus let it go,
and blossom on to each page as you know.

Love is found in these poems.
To the authentic you:
let your Light Work shine through; commence and create,
to be true to you.

INTRODUCTION

It was in a moment that created itself, a combination of mysterious coincidences that birthed a sense of connection, that Lotus Lifting was gifted to me through my guardian angel - in a time that I had lost the power to hear myself anymore.

After heartbreak, struggling as a single mother and my business decreasing - due to my decision to follow my true path - I had lost all hope. Nevertheless, in that moment of total surrender, a voice began channelling through me. I lay in the bath thinking: how could it have come to this? Almost everything in my life had been stripped away from me. Thank goodness I had my two beautiful sons there. This is what I give thanks for, and I'll continue to do so for the rest of the days I'm lucky enough to be able to say: I'm their mother.

I started writing my thoughts down and they reverberated through me in a way which I'd not experienced before. Almost like a waterfall of energy, flowing into streams of consciousness with messages of purity, love and an idea to trust the elements of emotional poetry. In ten months, I had written over one hundred poems and felt it was time to share these thoughts with the world, with you.

It was this experience that brought me to an epiphany of self-worth. For the past six years I have been searching for myself. I fell in and out of abusive relationships, being bullied as a child, in my relationships and work environment. There were a lot of pieces that needed to be found, let alone put together, as the jigsaw puzzle that was my life just never seemed to fit right. After the boys' father left, I decided, enough is enough. I threw myself into my self-development, in order to become a woman that I could be proud of. I said no to the anti-depressants and yes to meditation, holotropic breathing and Native American medicines like Kambo, Ayahausca and Cacao.

Work had to be done to access the soul and from these ventures and losing the loves of my life in the process, I found Lotus Lifting. I found my purpose by working through methods of love, including Therapy Poetry, Mindful Light Work practices and Reiki healing.
Each poem was channelled with the support of the Universe and Mother Nature. Each song of the soul has an individual meaning to every reader,

helping to heal or access an emotion. There are seventeen elements which discuss spiritual meditation and natural awareness as part of a journey to assist you in your development to consciousness. I hope by reading this, that it provides you with the key to unlock the mind. I found it through pure vulnerability, joyful growth and abundant love, all of which I had to utilize to craft my writing.

After my journey to Peru and a spiritual awakening at Machu Pichu, I felt as if things were shifting. It was like I had done a 180 degree turn from my previous experience of the world; I became more connected to my existence yet could label and distance myself from the negative areas of my life. So I said goodbye to high heels and nights of not remembering, in exchange for books, courses, enlightened peoples and a connection to meditation, which seemed to happens so quickly yet so effortlessly.

I furthered my spiritual connection through life coaching, crystal healing, colour therapy and sound healing. These blessings sent ripples of pure positivity into my life. I entered Reiki, which has now become my way of life, and I am proud to say that today I am a Reiki Master Teacher so I can attune others to heal with the honour of the universal energies. I also achieved a distinction in meditation and mindfulness. I wish to progress with my teachings, and this book is one way of doing so, helping to serve through words, feelings and energy in order to heal, as we are one and when we expand in love we nourish all that we surrender to the higher self. I sincerely hope you find some of this love within the pages of Lotus Lifting.

Life isn't easy and the path can be rocky, nevertheless, when we face what we need to, we heal. Only then can we truly experience what life has to offer.

To begin, I also want to thank Abraham Hicks for being there when I thought no-one else was listening. This consolidation has been aided and so beautifully received and appreciated.

Today is the gift,
tomorrow isn't granted.
So, lift dear lotus, into the world,
raise your flower up to be seen,
and unfold your petals of persona.
You are so special,
so perfect in every way,
the world is waiting to see you.
So, grow baby, in your own special way.

HOW TO ACCESS ELEMENTAL POETRY

The Poetry has been channelled on a therapeutic frequency and must be accessed in this way. This way we can really connect with the emotional elements after sitting with the words and letting them vibrate through the cells. It allows healing by allowing you to invite a spiritual song in order to create a harmony with your higher self.

Each therapeutic poem is a length that we can connect with. The poems carry emotional messages which you should access via a meditative ritual each time you open the book in order to gain the maximum from it. Firstly, think of how you are feeling and use this to select an elemental chapter. For example, if you want to shine then 'Light' may be a good choice. Secondly, find your place of solace, a space in which you can be with yourself and be as present as possible; your pose can be sat cross-legged, lain down on your bed or sat up you're your spine aligned with both feet placed on the floor and your head upright to receive the universal love. When comfortable, breath in through the nose and receive the cool air that nourishes every moment of your existence then exhale the warm air back to the Earth, your home, your paradise.

Now that you are grounded and ready for the words to attune your vessel for mindful rebalancing, read the divine poetry slowly and carefully take in each word of the elemental poem you have matched with.

Now close your eyes and sit with those words, allow any feeling. You are perfect for this space in time. When you're ready, come around slowly, adjust and be grateful for the appreciation of self and the time you have made in order to grow, to develop, to heal, to be.

These beautiful practices are on the page, waiting for you anytime and anywhere. As long as you have a copy of Lotus Lifting you can be fully awakened to the source of your higher self to aid any residual healings that you feel want to be recognised.

Lotus, it's time to shake the mud off and spread those unique petals of you, as you are here for reasons that the universe scripted. So, shine, share and create an eternal love of you.

"As you think thoughts that feel good to you, you will be in harmony with who you really are"

Abraham Hicks.

Element One

Release.

"go for it now, the future is promised to no one."

Wayne Dwyer.

Stars Shelter

Sometimes,
just sitting and listening to the sounds of rain on a roof
can remind you that you have shelter.

Remember,
the feelings were because so much love was there,
remember that you are true love
and eternally loved.

Remember,
that a smile is worth more than money,
a helping hand is more important than one that rubs your ego,
and a courageously compassionate conversation is priceless.

For when we are brought to our knees,
this is when we have to look up,
and even though the daylight is overcast,
the storm will clear,
the blue will calm
and the stars always follow.

So, dazzle in your dance
of being on Mother Earth
without rhythm or reason,
for you are the only one
who decides what your worth truly is.

The Whisper in the Wind

Whilst the wind will never surrender,
it's strength still has a whisper of wonder,
the hours of past hurt are only in the air.
You can't see them anymore.

The reality of the new realms of what will fade into a withering gale
has taken away your pain.

For all we have is now,
so hold on.
Even when it blasts from the sky,
in to an ever endless unknown,
for you are the truest soul.

From heart and solace just let it go,
to play with the breeze as the storm has passed.
You are free from hanging on.

No more tycoons will treat your beauty with harm,
the heavens will open your heart to who you really are.

Mermaid's Tales and Shipwrecks

Building up.
Only to have to let it all go.
Like the ocean deep it has another world beneath the waves.

Like an orchestra of obstruction,
you must ride your own way through it.
It may be destructive,
but only then can you find the calm.

The shore is inevitable.
But to race to get there
would waste away the tales of shipwrecks old,
and mermaids filled with pure pleasure.

For peace can be found in danger and love in tides.
Keep your current and let it take you,
into the unexpected sands of time.

When we Shone

Where are you my love?
I smell your scent in the air,
I see your smile through the leaves
of the forest.

The woods are filled with trails of our footsteps,
of pure divine love,
and in the leaves lie
past conversations filled with laughter.

Can we not dance in the rain together?
Glow in the sun as we entangle into one?
Why my Earth angel did this have to be done?

To protect is to liberate,
But to guard is to smother.
So, Let your beast slumber dear.

Life is a mix of messages,
so, keep it clear.

Let the tragedy end,
stop reliving a life that has gone.
Come make some more memories of when we shone.

Pride with You

To the spirits with the lion's mane,
don't be tamed.

This life has made the most out of your past.
The other side of the coin is coming,
your next move is going to change your reality.

Flip it
Feel it
Fill it.

Lioness, you have your pride with you.
No more will pain hunt you,
for you are the predator of the purest form.

Seek your Serengeti,
peace is coming,
allow your soul to rest.

So, don't stress,
take your time,
that is when your pride will shine.

Pleasure Spent

Unchaining the changeable that was put in place,
to lose a love that was sent for good.

For pleasures spent,
love now wars on some other plain.
So, let it go and rise above from your pity domain.

For this is now and this is pure, everything can change.
Your true love sent,
just opened up –
they are on the midnight train.

Listen to the mystic moon,
feel through the light vibration.
Write your offerings and take your time to get to your final destination.

Bby Girl

Bby girl why are you still hurting?
This pain isn't yours to carry,
the pasts are no longer here.

I know it hurts;
it rips your heart,
but please don't tear yourself apart.

No more messages of deep regret,
for a place you wanted to forget.

You can't shape yourself in someone else's vision.
So, be strong in your will and mission.

Your day is coming you know it's true.
Stop making up stories that were never you.

Vibration in Bloom

For the anger is the passion:
the love and frustration,
of the partner who is the only one that wants to be seen,
for the girl needs to cut the old obscene.

This chapter needs to close before the real fairytale will begin.
For the past will untie this love so true,
that entangles the heart
that only happens for a few.

You know when love has honour and is true,
so, trust in the words and find the new obsession in bloom.

Open up,
like the lotus you truly are,
wider and taller for this is the only form,
in which you can become
bigger and more beautiful than ever before.

When you listen to the words that your soul applauds,
be humble and bow.
This is the time the magic will appear.

So, flourish dear woman into the queen that you are.
Open up,
for this time you're not far.

Wild like the Waters

The words are the magic,
the thoughts of the unpure that sit in the underbelly of fear.
These are the scriptures that set the story.

The tellers of friendship,
that maybe of selfish nature,
they want to keep the love caged and corrupted.

Still this beast will not be tamed,
as its love is wild like the waters.
A melancholy of crystal-clear clarity,
that can evolve into the most powerful riptide of passion.
Pulling you in with no control,
nevertheless we all know the secret is,
to just let go.

For when we allow the wave to take us,
we can then reach our golden sands.

To lie with the love,
on many platforms of pleasure,
that star-crossed souls will only experience.

As time is only made by man.
Still love is always there,
strong like the beast that has no fear.

The Taste of Temptation

Temptations too good to only take a taste.
Nevertheless, when you have had your fill of delicacies,
release the feast as it is only greed.

The inner nourishment is the only real fruition.
Where we spoon in the fruits of Gia, of others and self.

To dine in passion, surrender, diligence and virtue.
This is the experience that tells you when you feel full.

So, take from the table and pull up your pew.
But be careful who you share your plate with,
as they must repay with the pure,
not the processed.

Clear away the delicious seduction.
Take a piece of the peace,
allow the celebration with the source
of opulent endless release.

The Lost Poem

Sweet Goodbye.
Let it go.
All the memories made for that time only caused dismay -
a soul of lies who will never awake.

Two spirits that won't ever create.
One was pure passion, and the other, a pure pretender.
For the shows weren't real,
besides,
all stories must come to an end.

For now, you are free to truly be,
so, don't live like before
and pass the time on the idle abyss of unsure.

For love is eternal,
and that can't be passed by,
as this is the story of your sweet goodbye.
The one that never was,
the one that dives into deep dishonesty to keep the lies alive.

The Hummingbird Prose

To hold onto anything for too long makes us grow tired. Even as simple a task as holding a glass of water upright, causes the arm to tire. Sometimes, even the simplest of tasks becomes difficult if you do them for long enough. To release your anxiety isn't as hard as you may think, as this is only a stored energy. When you know how to release it you can be free to fly again. Nevertheless, having the knowledge and practices to let go of unhelpful energies is a responsibility and a task you need to take care of. Like that glass of water, you can only hold so much of that life-giving medicine before it starts spilling over and making a mess.

Keep your glass full but don't let it spill out everywhere. The damp rots if it isn't wiped away.

The hummingbird meditation title of the next practice was gifted to me whilst I was on a spiritual trip around Peru. This is where my first spiritual conscious shift happened - I was that glass, and a waterfall of past experiences and low vibrations had drowned me in anxiety.

In the Peruvian Manu Rainforest I woke up to the knowledge that I could not go to see the cliff birds of Peru, something I had been looking forward to. I had to rest and release, I lay in the secluded rainforest surrounded by so much beauty that it seemed intrinsic to all aspects of life. I lay in an opening of flowers and baby pineapples and meditated. When I came around, I heard a humming: scores of hummingbirds surrounded me, and I then became present. I could finally feel and see the beauty.

I knew I was exactly where I was meant to be, on my own missing out on the adventure to find my one path. The beauty and the unexplained vibrant frequency of these birds was one of the most beautiful sights I have ever witnessed.

This was a reminder, that even in your wildest and most incredible moments of reality, you must remain as one to enjoy the moment. In this release we can find our return to soul and appreciation.

This is why the hummingbird meditation is your first Light Work meditation. So that your beautiful wings will never get weighed down. So that you are ready to finally access a free and enlightened state, despite it existing during your every moment, lifetime and shift of your experience.

The Hummingbird Meditation

Begin with finding a calm place where you won't be disturbed, sit down, cross legged with your spine in a straight position, or laying down in a Shavasana pose.

Set a timer. From 5 minutes for beginners, to 30 for those experienced with hummingbird breath work.

Start by slowly closing your eyes. If you prefer, a light gaze at a fixed object will work. Now start inhaling through your nose. Feel the cold air coming in through your nasal passages and filling your chest. When you're ready, release and concentrate on the warmth of the air that your lungs have produced when exhaling. Repeat this natural rhythmic breath for 10 rounds.

Now, after you inhale the air that fills your body with the life giving force (known as chi or in other cultures Prana energy) on the exhale begin to hum through your nasal passage, until all of the air feels as if it has depleted.

RELEASE

REPEAT THIS FOUR TIMES

Now fill the body with the inhalation. Start filling your belly, your lungs, and your head space, counting to ten with each round of your breathwork cycle. Make sure it feels comfortable, you may want to alter the number of repetitions to help with this. Exhale again until the breath has left your lungs.

REPEAT THIS TEN TIMES

Fall into a relaxed state of natural breath and end when you desire.

After your practice write down how you felt before the practice?
How did the breath work go for you?
How do you feel now?

This will cement the sequence of release, and also act as a reminder as to why it is so important to keep checking in with yourself - to feel free as the hummingbird.

Element Two

Soul.

"you are soul, and you are love not a spirit or an angel or a human being!"

Rumi.

Guide of your Mind

Sitting in a bubble of bewilderment and boundaries,
the pain of pleasures that could be, cause unease.

The whisper from a message you don't want to forget,
to protect what you are becoming,
you heard it in the autumn breeze.

"I haven't seen you in forever!",
"How are you my love?",
Hold this message close and remember,
you are adored.

Time has stood still.
Write the words,
connect the energies,
fall into a rapture of Love's tendencies.

You can laugh, learn,
and become the guide of your mind.
But just remember this all takes time.

Space to Wander

Running from your own skin,
ever a distraction and a fear.
To release into you is the only truth.

Running from thoughts that remain clear and pure,
they are you:
the many others that think as one.

The madness movement will always be there,
accessing the reasons for this is the way,
the messages can flow through your veins.

In your mind the clarity can be found,
it's in the listening that happens from underground.

So, come out of the outer world,
of collisions of wonder.

You are many forms of Love and Source,
and this has given you time,
and space,
to wander through the lives of many.

So, come on and sit with me.
Let it be.

Rapture of Sisterhood

Love doesn't have to be the way you have been taught;
it can be a rapture of sisterhood,
a love of infinite power.

For the girls have lived on many levels,
from the oldest souls these two star-seeds,
were always meant to meet.

In places they felt they shouldn't be were the lessons.
But the reason for this love of a lifetime connection is to find oneself.

The two soul sisters that skip through galaxies,
into another frequency,
as they possess the secrets to the magic.

They will only allow a passion and purity of the energy to rest within,
moving into the knowledge that they are love,
and they are always in love.

Hear the Wounds

For the days of ignorance cannot just be filtered out,
as the whispers became sirens of the inner search.

So, seeker,
hear the wounds and listen to heal,
for today is the only time you will feel the pain.
For Source is trusting and knows what is best.

So, waste no moments with stress,
as you are a miracle.
Just be, chill and rest,
for this is the next season to reinvest.

Though the leaves will drop,
they will turn to gold.
So, let this be a reminder,
letting go is another way to mould.

Claw the Ritual

Take away the inspection:
the rules that society have created,
the behaviour of the inceptions –
that introvert the extrovert.

Pass the levels,
go way back and claw the ritual,
as the mother will always be here as your soul
and Source knows.

Be the one that can be at one,
with the spirit guides that have left the messages in the other dimensions.

The platforms of patience and purge,
the place of complete surrender,
this is when you face your mirror.

With the guides of galaxies,
the intimacy with self,
will grow into relationships of love and strength.

So, writer,
keep creating and loving the others that come from the stars,
because we are all here to find our shine.

Into the Blue

As you fly into the blue,
let all the clouds of coincidence connect with each wing,
and allow a message to the soul.

Of pure passion, pleasure and peace,
for the horizon is near,
the lands of love are there to be ventured.

Through the sands of sensuality,
the mountains of strength,
and the landscapes of loyalty;
the fires in the distance glow brighter.

As we step closer,
the soul knows the sky.
It tells the soul to dance:
we are more than our physicality.

Fly,
be free to open up into you,
feel the feelings,
speak your truth.

Screen of Life

Baby Queen,
take your time to display your dream,
the screen of life can keep you switched into lives of lies.

Make sure you follow your heart,
and find the likes that truly love you,
not only in the dream state,
but reality.

Move the magic in your mind maiden,
don't let it go to scroll,
on endless pages of empty content,
that has no soul.

Find your space and keep it real,
within this story you will reveal,
the other Universe of spirit blessed.

This is real and don't ask why,
just keep the requests to get those dreams,
out of the screens,
of your dreams.

We Are One

Wake and see the world,
in all its beauty and raise for peace.

Shine you lights,
hold on tight,
because we are one,
and when we come together,
this is when it's done.

Cast out all the evil,
but do not forget:
this is the constant reminder,
of what we have to protect.

Rise up in soul connection,
in peace and compassion,
because we are the divine,
the ones who love without rhythm or rhyme,
for just the moments, not the greed.

All life is precious: wouldn't you agree?
All sons and daughters should have time to breath.
So, rise up sweet spirit and guide others with light,
because this is the new world with all its delights.

The Woman on the Outside

Remember the women you really are,
the one who is your soul.

The woman on the outside,
that inspires and keeps it cool.
The one who is living her experience,
with vision and fuel.

To give to others without a second thought,
with love just running through every molecule.

So just do you dear womankind,
remember this is not a dual this time,
release the ghouls and realise,
your outside light is also deep inside.

Priestess of Power

For the shifts she had to realign,
it was written in the stars:
the Priestess of Power.

Her ability to make you feel love with one look,
her drive of the pursuit of truth,
is brave and strong.

For her messages need to be heard:

We are one.
We are awake.
We shall not wait.
We all matter.

With her energy she will transform as her clan have spoken,
and the gift of healing humanity is transformed, as:

We are one.
We are awake.
We shall not wait.
We all matter.

The Fire Vision Prose

Your soul is something you can't see, or touch, in a physical reality. Nevertheless, we know it's there - your very own navigational system to connect you via your energy to your higher purpose.

The soul is your essence; like fire it has its own way of moving and feeling. The candle, the wood, the coal, are the objects that fire chooses to weave its tales of the elemental. Much like your wonderful body, the vessel that has been gifted to you and is perfect in its creation, for every segment of your life.

The soul is the fire that the body feels can burn you, if you don't respect it's message. Yet it's a brave, beautiful light that enlivens your energetic and physical sides.

The Fire Vision Meditation

To begin the soul-connective Fire Vision practice, you will need to have: a candle and a lighter, a peaceful environment and allow time to settle into the practice.

Fire is the closest thing to sunlight; the frequency of the flames stimulates the third eye with nourishing wavelengths of light. Fire Vision is the practice of watching fire in a gazed vision. In this practice, a candle is being used, but if you have a log burner or a fire, this can enhance the visuals, as the fire allows itself to weave its magic on a greater scale.

Firstly, light your candle and have it in a safe place. (Sitting at your desk or around a table is a safe space to create for your practice.)

Now, sit on a chair, or cross legged - just make sure your spine is in a straight elevated posture, with the crown of your head ready to receive from the energy above you. Place your hands on your thighs, palms facing up to receive the life force energy that surrounds you in every moment. Your feet should be flat on the ground if sitting down. Take your shoes off for more connection to mother Earth.

Now, inhale deeply through your nose, and breath out with an audible sigh as your exhaling cycle. Continue this breathing for four rounds.

Now, take your breath to an organic rhythmic flow and softly zone your vision into the flame, gaze don't look, a soft sight will access the calm to connect with your soul. Gaze naturally - you can blink, just relax and home in on how the fire does its own thing, without judgement, instruction or structure.

This Fire gazing should last around 15 minutes in order to allow you to release control of what you may have been experiencing that day.

When you feel you are ready, blow out the candle. Now close your eyes and breath - inhaling the scents around you. Slowly open your eyes and take time to reflect on your practice, journaling any emotions, questions or breakthroughs, as in reflection we can see what we may need to.

Soul connecting allows us to feel freer, connect to calmness and restore energy.

Element Three

Surrender.

"We can never make peace in the outer world until we make peace with ourselves"

Dalai Lama.

Cutting Cry

When you can't let it out
and it holds so tight,
through the tremble in your throat,
that feels like ice.

The cutting cry that aches for days,
why can't we go our separate ways?
To be loved for who we are.

Don't change the star you are,
but hold back from shooting every time,
to stop you getting lost in space and time.

The dullness that can't ever accumulate,
that will only hold you to stagnate,
and rot in waste.

For the words that come from you,
have only ever been:
holy,
sincere
and true.
Don't let the others dim your story.

Shine sweet starlet;
be strong and proud,
for you are beautiful,
brave,
and love is all around.

The Stolen Voice of a Mermaid

Now you may not understand.
When someone is not allowed to be who they are,
and when their time comes,
they will dive deep into themselves and never resurface.

For this little mermaid,
who was starved on land,
her dream of love was an entrapment,
that caused her to lose her authentic voice.

The other world:
the Odyssey with undercurrents of creativity,
was the only fruitful reality,
she ever wanted to live in.

In her cave of all the things she loved,
which were never physical,
for she was surrounded by the feelings that she touched.

So, this became her duty;
to fill the cave with energies,
to brighten up her soul,
a song of healing,
some words for the spirits and self-expression,
to show her true inner beauty.

For her happiness was found in the trinkets and shrines,
of other times and futures,
that had yet been told.

For now, she will live in the moment,
and not the times of sands,
free to swim to shallows
of surrender and success.

Sweet Source

Go explore this journey,
take isolation,
make connections,
and honour the revilement of your truth,
which may not give rest.

We lose people from our flock,
but then like birds of a feather we align,
and fly.
To soar together, with the ones who dare to take to the skies.

Because we are what we are,
and are never alone.
Sweet Source we know you are there,
with guidance pure and old.

So, fly into the sky
to find those ancient soaring souls.

Inhumane

I can't remember when it was.
I could really have no pain,
As they say in time it goes away.
But this feels like it's so inhumane.

To mould and fix yourself,
to be someone else's life,
has took away the sanity -
and bit by bit your life.

Let it go,
become unshackled
from life's lustful hurricane.

Take away the chains,
to let that person be free in your heart.
Take away the endless drain,
of when you thought you had the one:
the ever-endless flame.

Speak to the Blue Moon

Stop eating yourself up,
with that tainted lust,
it will never be enough.
Just wait, and be patient to let others in.

Ones that love,
without the threat of taking away.
Ones that see magic,
and not hearsay.

For your mind is yours,
and true with creativity.
Whereas the other half is painted with tragedy,
the ghouls of old will always live there,
don't look back at the past -
it isn't there.

Sweet soul, look forward with vision,
and smite the monster that tried to win the battle.
That soul was marked for a different purpose.

A purpose of ego,
not light,
for the others let them walk into the dark.
You dear spirit tried with all of your might,
but let go now,
before it takes your shine.

So, set the fire and burn the past,
ask for the love that will always last;
creative, supportive, honourable and true.

Speak to the blue moon,
just make a wish for you.

Not your Fairytale

To lose is to put the quest into someone else's power,
this can never bring the treasure
that only rests inside of you.

Time is irrelevant,
the love is the only thing that is real,
Other duels that lead them to a path of thrill seeking
will never be enough.

So why listen dear spirit?
As you are awake,
allow the princesses to sleep,
it is the only way they will have their fairytale.

A kiss to break the slumber of society's rules
is a blessing you can only find when you put your trust in the soul.

The soul that is connected to the Source,
the stars,
the moon
and all the magic created through many manifestations.

The Surrender of our State

Walking with the water will reveal
the inner wavelengths of the obstructed physical,
the deep and calculated cavernous core.

For as the water passes through the layers of humanity
it is the same for the Earth.

Those who were in a purgatory,
a place of war of the internal elements,
have now escaped all judgements.
For why would the most beautiful of souls,
have to take a role
in this charade of human games?

They take each quake to only become stronger,
grounded by their knowledge and blessings.

The medicines of nature find the inner belonging.
As this is Pacha Mama,
and when we share this world
this is the only time we can authentically create.

Create into vision,
time and space.
Invite the surrender of our state,
keep the knowledge running deep
through the magma of the pathway's gates.

Pause and Replay

Don't press fast forward.

Please baby girl,
take your time
to have peace in your slumber
and your soul's respect.

Move forward with grace.
Take your time to pause and replay,
but don't stay
or stop,
or skip,
because to get to the good parts,
even the scenes where hands cover eyes need to play out.

Don't stop that shout out moment,
sit with the action Queen,
be the innovator and creator
of conscious content.

Queens still reign without their King,
just make sure you do so with
pride,
purity
and power.
For the commitment of love's next episode.

A Beautiful Lie

What a beautiful lie you've created,
with visions and talks of love
and endless time.

To take away someone's heart is unjustified,
but there is hope in tragedy.
I will thrive in the cracks
that broke my trust.

This defeat is not mine but yours to carry,
for the lack of trust has
Eaten your good alive,
and left an empty shell
seeking others to fill that shallow space.

I will love in the solace of peace and dignity but with courage at Source.
I'm so grateful you have set me free.

You treated me with a life laced with lies.

I hope you can wake and rise,
into the spirit you disguise.

The Let Go List practice

To surrender is the only way we can begin to let go of what isn't serving us, it is the freeing of one's life experience. It's the knowledge that we can only control the controllable and we must surrender the uncontrollable before it starts to affect us in an unhealthy way.

A practice that can help with this is the let it go list. This is a list with two sides that you title:

WHAT I CAN CONTROL

&

WHAT I CAN'T CONTROL

When overwhelming thoughts of tasks, times and emotions come over us, we can sometimes worry about things we can't do anything about, like the behaviour and choices of others.

That is why the 'Let Go' list is a great visual releasing tool to tap into the secret of soothing yourself. The list dictates the things I can achieve if I choose to act on them seriously. Then erase the uncontrollable list as this is not worth your energy.

So, surrender and allow yourself to let go if nothing can be done about it. If it is irrelevant, you just need to get it out of your mind in order to see that sometimes these things really don't matter that much. So rather than allowing your mind to fill up with pressures which you can't do anything about, flip it. Act on what you can, in order to get that list done, don't let your mind take you off of your path. Number the jobs in your 'What I can control' list in the order in which you would like to complete them, then gently flow through these tasks in order to enrich the feeling of staying on track.

Don't rush it! Remember that being mindful at all times is the key to a partnership with your higher self.

Element Four

Resurrection.

"The symbolic language of the crucifixion is the death of the old paradigm; resurrection is a leap into a whole new way of thinking"

Deepak Chopra.

Dear Starlight

Sit in starlight dear girl, for the nightmare is over.
From the dawn you were different and so misunderstood.

This is your last night,
the last night pretending,
the last night of obstacles.

For the next time darkness falls,
you will release into the reality of the Universe within you.
For its beauty has been moulded through tragedy.

When the essence of impurity
has withered and dripped at your soul for too long,
trust in the mother
and the mother you are,
as you are worthy of love
and you are loved.

So, live with every cell that has a message of past life,
for beauty is different
and you don't have to hide.

No more pity for the other side,
they will never understand.
Yet this is ok,
for if we all aligned the truth could not be discovered.

So, shine dear starlight,
your story is one of another world and time,
just be you,
justly divine.

You Never Betrothed

To the boy who used to be the Universe,
the soul with so much love.
There was no other alike.

For the years were hard,
and your story was of heartache.
The lessons you were given,
you decided to reject.

All of the tears you made,
yet I wasn't allowed to cry.
I tried to breath a word of expression,
but suppression was your masterplan.

In your world there are divides,
and those kind eyes now only have a vision of evil.
For the beauty lies within the beholder,
and you never betrothed.

Your diction is not true to others,
and I have torn down your direction.
For our lives are our own and not there to manipulate.

Your relationships are in your heart,
and the ones that speak truth
will always nurture the voice.

For now, I am the one with the words of wisdom.
Thank you, old Universe,
for the bruises and cracks,
as this is the only way I could see my truest beginning.

The Beauty and the Bull

He played here once,
your lover man with fantasy and excitement.
Covering this life span, of dreams of mountains and inner peace.

Still there were lies he created in his own head
to push out love.
Yet nonetheless
he just dreaded the hurt instead.

To shove away a woman who shone,
was a decision that the darkness won;
for he was a spirit with two sides.

A bull of stubborn pride who raged on fear.
The beast could not hide,
but when the tempered subside,
the angel is there to find.

With caring kind loving eyes,
and arms like wings to wrap you in,
helps you forget the past pain within.

This is the story of the beauty and the bull:
a love that could never be done but will always exist.

True love will take time and patience,
so, take your place until your stubborn beast makes up its mind.

Chameleonic Dreams

When the heart aches like it has for days,
though patience turns to anxiety,
she awaits the lover's call.

For she is one who is ready to change,
her life has been a chameleonic dream,
of everchanging colours and streams.

Existing in the pain
she will heal.
She will listen to the ancestry in her veins,
the family she has,
the friends that make her whole.

She won't let this evolution be stolen
by the jealousy that sears the tongues of the lesser trusting,
for she is pure in each resurrection.

To only be loved is her quest,
And surely this has been addressed,
for love is her vibration,
and will never be a test.

So, walk on the scales of the colours quest
and realise that this is the rest.

The Beat of a Message

Even though the times are tough,
To create is the tonic that eases the torn heart.

As words fall out of a soul that is confused
with the partner's ego and destruction,
the writer will go on.

She feels the pain,
she sees the gift
and slides into a space of unease
to create the beauty.

As it beats with a message of the direction of duty,
she must take the pressure,
as this will be released when the words are done.

Letters that enable the love of self,
and that remove the smoke and mirrors.
When the full stop hits the last page,
the past is gone.

Secrets We Kept

In letting you go,
I learnt that I loved you on another level,
for the secrets we kept
crept into the light.

The space that now divides
we honour with support and respect, as the growth has to come from
oneself.

A pair that was as old as stars,
lived in realms of the most authentic connection.

As we are apart, we grow together,
for time is a healer and it will only show
that which appears on the next flow.

Serendipity Sisters

The soul sisters that see in serenity,
the two sunshine souls who stroll through seamless searching.

For these two spirits have met worlds over and are always in eternity,
they enrapture the love of Source.

By surrendering to soul
their heart's healing is the manifestation
which became the magic.

For the mountain kin of integrity,
these sirens wont rest.
Still they feel for what they can see in emotion and trust.
As the day has now turned into an everlasting peaceful dusk.

Find Your Way Lover

Let the Universe find your way lover,
it's time for you to heal and deal in other matters,
for the love we shared
was always in the past.

Life is too short lover and we all have dreams,
so if they don't align,
they can't become complete.

Love was all I wanted - just joy and time,
with endless nights of passion
and days of pure sublime.

Nevertheless, this attraction was not made to last
and now it has been denied.

For a King needs a Queen,
but this one won't deny
the promise of a princess,
that reaches out to love
all that ends at the heavenly skies.

And so, the special day will have to reign forth,
for the castle and clan to remain.
If we wait,
it will stagnate
and fade away
till it has found Source.

Sweet girl

Sweet girl this is true bliss,
Sweet girl you have your loved one
In your arms right now:
this is the only moment that exists.

So sweet girl don't reminisce,
be kind,
be true
and sweet girl remember,
this can only be done by you.

Don't fear,
don't cry
because sweetest girl you have you
and that is now your true bliss.

Release the others that don't serve you,
remember you are perfect and loved by yourself
and your Universe
sweet girl.

Move Mountains

For having your head too far into the clouds
can cause you to forget
what you have right in-front of you.

The love of someone so special
that changed every emotion into strength and confidence,
for this was once the one I thought I would get lost with
in time and space forever.

By wandering through those dreams with you,
I would find myself lost.
After so long sleeping under the stars,
I couldn't stand out and shine bright.

For the gifts of the Universe have always been wrapped in one lover.
These weren't twin flames,
it was the suppression of the inner child,
the protector of her power.

The love was the only element which was real,
and when this is found inside,
this is when you can move your emotional mountains.

A Gentle Touch Practice

To resurrect into our own authentic soul, you must remind yourself how special you are, and how perfect you have always been. You have existed like this in every sequence of your life, and you need an awareness of this to be kinder to yourself.

This Light Work practice, the Gentle Touch, is one where we connect with the physical self; the biomechanical suit you were gifted with when you arrived on this Earth. Your bodily vessel is a beautiful piece of artistry, and the way we interact with it has an effect on our soul.

So, with that in mind, when we become conscious and connect to the feelings of unhelpful thought about our bodies, if any part of your perfect vessel isn't feeling as aligned as you think it should be, show it love, pour mental thoughts of gratitude and touch to the areas.

For example, you could be in the shower washing. This is a perfect time to touch the skin with gentle touch: be it your legs, arms, stomach or face, give it love - a tender touch, stroke or even give yourself a hug for a minute.

Do this every day, once in the morning and then in the evening. Your vessel needs that love as much as you do, your cells are listening. Likewise, if someone were unkindly to you with thoughts or physical actions, then this may not make you feel good. Your body needs that affection and compassion, so take the time and be gentle. Then you will be able to step into your higher self and be present in the life you truly deserve.

Element Five

Desire.

"The moment you become aware of your desires you can easily see that no desire can be filled"

Osho

Sides of Me

Showing you all the sides of me creates a tapestry
of enchantment and desire,
for we can be who we want to be.

To design myself for you is a treat I savour,
like the sweet kiss that ignites my body with burning pleasure.

The acts of love we create,
only validate
the need to be with you,
in every way I can possibly be.

So, let's play for eternity
and create the scene we want to be in,
as we are the directors of this love.

Tender Touch

The love we create daily is a sea of sensitive seduction,
an intimacy that few will ever feel in a lifetime.

As I undress my soul to you,
you heal my body in ways I never knew were real,
this love connection is your magic.

The tender touch that heals so many exhausting experiences,
became a tonic of adoration
that I reciprocate in sensuality and sincerity.

For the love of a lifetime has to be earned,
and I offer myself to you in my raw naked form,
in physical and spiritual incarnation.

Dark Side of Me

To look but not to touch was a test of the dark side of me.
I had to hold back to be able to connect with you angelically.

As we mix in moments of ecstasy,
we find ourselves through each other
and soar into the night with the trust of each other.

I let you in bit by bit gritting my teeth still with incredible pleasure,
as you are the one who gives me the purest release.

Through the body,
mind
and spirit,
a new vibration is being created
that only the twin flames will experience.

A Moth to a Flame

The language of love that drips off your tongue
entices me like a moth to a flame.

The burn of a wing which set alight
and enlivens the night
with irreplaceable pleasure.

For when the space is created,
we can revive a magic
that has lived in our souls for a thousand years.

Like the hunger of a predator that needs their fill to survive,
your touch possesses the same ability and I obey your every will.

So, chain my love with our true blood connection
and make a mad love that will last an eternity.

Sacred Fires

You reach me like the sun hitting my body,
warming up each cell with light and radiance,
for when you touch me,
I set on fire.

To desire each exchange from a time that you looked away,
has now become a mirror that aligns the two flames that fight a sacred fire.

A ceremony of a tantric connection
flows with a purity and passion that stings
and has created a love of loins and co-creation.

So, keep moving into me
and we will eclipse into a dark desire
that creates a whole consciousness of intensity.

Waiting in the Stars

A request that can't be denied,
like the night sky waiting in the stars to shine,
you will always be mine.

From the moment you saved me I wanted to be in your arms,
forever becoming one in the sheets,
like the sea moving for the hunter moon.

Building up with a sweet serenity,
a taste so sweet that intoxicated the senses
and leaves one wanting more.

The elements within the lovers,
the sheer heat that sets the limbs on fire
with creativity at Source.

The trust to allow you to take me to a new space within me,
as I know you will never let go.
So, have all of me.
Mind body and soul.

Be the first to have every little bit of me,
even the worse twists
that turn our bond into one that can never be undone.

Brighter than the Northern Star

When you love me like a woman,
I feel vulnerable like a baby.
A trust with so much necessity of love from you.

When you hold me in your arms,
it's like you polish me into the most beautiful diamond
that shines brighter than the northern star.

I want to get lost with you in eternity,
for I feel like we will live forever
when we are together in our space.

Thank you for loving me like no other,
taking away all the fear from the past years
and creating a future that takes my breath away
with the beauty we create together.

Heat in my Heart

I surrender into every touch you want me to receive,
from passionate pleasure to pure patience.
The fire grows.

The heat in my heart and loins
fill with an energy that only you can release.
You are the twin flame.
The one that someone could find a lifetime searching for.

Fate created a story that told of before we intwined,
when the flames only seared the skin.

From childhood to a time where I thought you could never be mine,
nevertheless all good things come in time.

The burn that feels so sweet,
and only intensifies as our space grows.
The only way to keep the fire in control
is to come together in the secret of two souls experienced as one.

Love Like a Movie Scene

Love like a movie scene,
where you feel so much magic in the air
you become high on each other's chemistry.

A movement that can't be described,
for when we become one,
an outer body vibe is created.

Like we are being touched by the stars
and our togetherness is the secret of the Universe.

The love of two flames that are fireproof within each other's
mind, bodies, and souls.
To have always known you,
has been the love sold.

So, this is the tale of the artist and the writer,
and passion's storm created in the arms of the lovers.

Platonic to Symphonic

From platonic to symphonic,
the orchestra of a conduction of pleasure.
The enchantment begins to play.

Free flowing from the source of love,
like the trust the day gives the night -
two elements that will always remain.

As they pass each other in the enraptured sky,
they never lose sight of each other,
even when the stars shine brightly into their love vision.

Two different planes of mystery and light
that wait for the exchange in time,
for even though it's the finale,
the love will forever grow to show
this soulful piece in time.

Soul's Core

On the waters of uncontrollable feelings,
the sky beams into the sea with love instead of mistrust.

As the sun shines on the oceans,
warming the cold deep soul,
the waves become still and rested.

The energies of fire and water are opposite,
each working their own individual magic to feed the other.

So different, yet still finding ease in flowing from each other,
to reflect its beauty back to the sky
and to transcend the magic to the soul's core.

The partnership is as old as the Earth,
so, trust in the uncontrollable,
that is the only time when you can find pure ease.

Desire Dance Work

To desire too much can be unhealthy, the greed of man has taken over many souls and impure temptations can drain the soul of a true and authentic purpose. However, desire can also light up a soul: it can levitate one's mood, and, when we start to desire the right things, we start the path to health, happiness and well-being.

The Desire Dance work practice is an elevated movement, to connect us with our bodies as we respond to beats crafted with consciousness and Source. This Light Work is about losing your inhibitions, moving how you want to with no judgement - just your pure, authentic self.

You will need some music. This can be any genre you desire, but it is better if you pick one suited to your current mood.
Ask yourself these questions before deciding:

Do I need a pick me up?

Do I need to have a release?

Do I want to sit with a sad emotion?

Do I want to release anger?

Now that you have your music, find a space where you feel safe and have room to move. Start your music and take it in for around a minute

What can I hear?

How does it make me feel?

How does it make me want to move?

After this minute, start to move with just your senses guiding you. Dance how you want to feel in this moment.
Do this until the track or album is finished.

71

Now reflect on how you feel. Switch off the music and sit with yourself. This might only be for 30 seconds but allow your mood to move you and feel gratitude for that timeout.

Allow yourself to feel what you desired - what you wanted to let go of or receive.

Element Six

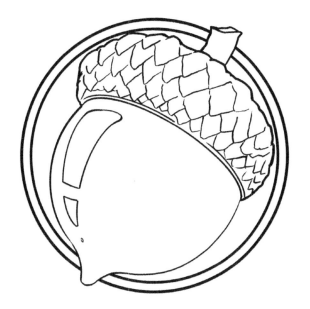

Growth.

"Every experience I have is perfect for my growth"

Louise Hay.

The Days are Bright

In the moments where the loneliest feelings live,
which slowly creep into the cracks of a heart broken by loves losses,
the solace is found within.

The only one you really have to love is yourself,
still listen to the words of loved ones.

Let go of useless patterns and thoughts of self-sabotage,
as this day is the gift,
and you must stay aware of all of your abundances.

The dark will always be there,
but Source will lead you back to the light with ease;
despite tests and the rest,
which show why life hasn't been so easy.

So, wake up world and join together.
As like the roots of trees that nourish each other in times of need,
we must take heed.

Be strong, compassionate, wholesome
and loved from the trunk of your solace
to the branches of your kin.

Rest assured the days are bright,
so take your time to grow into the light.

Ray of Source

For the things we don't see, hear or touch are the real emotions
and frequencies
that awaken the soul like a warm sunrise.

So, allow the ray of Source into every cell of brain,
body,
heart,
soul,
you.

Do we even know our own capabilities that we are all sent here to deliver?

Open the door of you,
like the Earth invites the next day,
don't be scared of what is written on the next page,
because you can't be anything but you.

So, shine those beams
that ignite intergalactic galaxies of your dark matter
that can never be explained.

Step into your full power - to be never understood,
but the creator of never-ending magic manifestation.

Senseless Seduction

Goodnight.
Enjoy the sweet slumber that is your endless night
of escaping and forcing love.

The magic is gone,
and now you have to live in the realm of the faded,
rot that is covered with fake gold
to hide many evils.

For the lover is on her own path now.
She has seen the light and escaped your cave of senseless seduction.

The enchantment is free to weave the layers of beauty and creativity
into another Light Work.

The beast had covered the treasure with layers of dirt so the enchantress
couldn't see her abundance,
but she has finally awoken to pursue peace in real life.

In the Space

As it's only in the space that the rest can be created,
realise the power that you have in you.

The love and connection are pure with others when you truly believe in
yourself,
for we are the gift,
the experience of eb and flow.

The waves will always crash in the emotions of your waters.
Nevertheless,
when we dive deep into the Source,
we find where the clarity exists.

Monsters of the under belly will still creep into your dreams,
yet our reality is the one we have control of.

The power to see all the treasures of friendship,
the chest may be locked for now,
but as the days pass the light starts to unlock.

So, when you see your riches,
don't let the greed set in.
The truth is that you have always been betrothed,
to all the materials of your unique abode.

Leaves of Insecurity

Air that moves through me,
like the sweet sea breeze that lingers on my leaves of insecurity.

For when the Earth and air meet,
the translation of the two happens without words.

Like the last rays of daylight
that go unnoticed,
that warm your soul with sunset sincerity
and embrace you even in solitude.

Keep running to that light as the present is all we have.

The twilight of our romance has begun,
and it is now or never;
our last day and night in which we can see who we really are.

Portal to You

As you pass over the lives which would have existed
if you had only decided to do things differently
and had the awareness of the real and the charade.

Many will try to pass the victory off as their own,
it will be their mistake.
Don't worry as through the integrity of others,
you will be able to see.

The fascination with life that you have to create –
make,
dream
and pour magic
into everything you do,
as your passions are the portal to you.

The door is only a façade,
the response only a perspective.

The purity is your choice,
so keep on feeling your way through the passage
till you find the purpose.
The now that just feels right,
because the door is always open,
for you to take flight.

Father and Friend

With kindness and strength,
he will push you on till the end.

The man that is a father to all his friends.

A wild and free spirit that
lives to love,
loves to live,
and is infinitely strong.

The man will always be
my friend,
my mentor,
my kindred spirit.

So, thank you,
oh, thank you,
for just being you dear king.

Little Lotus

Little lotus,
I know it can be hard this journey through the layers
to clear your sweet heart.

The more you travel,
the harder it may seem,
but dear flower remember,
you are creating your dream.

Each shift you conquer is where the roots grow,
they give you the stability
to really flow.

So, keep on going you are nearly there,
the sun is shining if you dare.
So sweet little lotus,
just take care,
for you are special,
far beyond anything anybody could compare.

Old Soul

To my sweet pea sister of the vine,
oh, how I thank you for our time,
for a soul connection so old
is hard to come by.

Your strength and compassion
flow each day,
and is the reason that the Universe made you my bae.

To shine your gifts bright and true,
to release into others that need you.
No matter what,
your passion will dictate for equality and peace.

I thank you for this my soul mate.

Layers of Design

Loving Lotus don't compare,
you will lose your enchantment if you dare,
keep your dream of you unique.

To unfold each blossom for that individual.
Dear flower,
your roots are strong don't be fooled.

You are travelling in your own sweet soul,
to the layers of design
that show the magnificence
that lived beyond the stars.

So, now you have landed on Earth
to plant and expand your passions of Source.
It's time to share this gift,
it's you.

So, keep on pushing with sweet ease,
this is your expedition on blessed Earth
and the blooms of love may go their separate ways,
nevertheless, stick to what your seedling has said,
uncover your magic and don't be led.

Appreciation Journaling

To grow in any part of your life it takes nurture and time. Like the beautiful willow that spends its time creating strong roots before it transcends into its elegantly strong beauty, we must also put in the work before we can grow to our full potential. Like the willow, you need patience to grow those roots, this can be aided by Appreciation Journaling. This will act as the roots that your mind needs in order to assist your spiritual evolution.

For this practice you will need a notebook to act as your journal - your place to gather your seeds of magic to start your own personal manifestation process. A good time to journal is before sleeping, as the roots you are putting in place will have more permanence to grow with time.

Start by writing down 10 things you have appreciated that day. These could be feelings, objects, people, concepts or music and anything in-between. Once you have written your feelings of gratuity on the pages, read the 10 lines out loud.

i.e.

I APPRECIATE MY FAITH IN GROWTH
I APPRECIATE MY COMFY BED
or
I APPRECIATE THIS TIME FOR SELF-REFLECTION BEFORE BED

These examples are just for reference.

When you write, read and vocalise your appreciation, they will nourish the soil of your mind, and for the rest of the night they can weave the magic of your own unique growth. Do this every night as it is an important Light Work for your development.

What are you are grateful for today?

Element Seven

Dark.

"Knowing your own darkness is the best method to dealing with the darkness of other people"

Carl Jung

The Shedding of Tears

The conflicts of a construction of cruelty can only be created
when trust is allowed to hurt the one you truly love.
This is a lesson in the relationship with self.

The lies that turn into laughter have to be untied,
as to twist and turn in raw emotions of insecurity,
can cut into the skin,
to show the pain you've allowed to silently grow.

The shedding of tears which reformed the soul to a new time,
and a pure relationship,
will give the strength to fight a past battle.

As time isn't the moments that man has taught you.
So, don't forget to say I love you before the next show.

Slip in Your Disgrace

The words you speak are only heard
by the ones still stuck in the moments we call hell.
As when you awake in our heaven
we can partner with the fire plain
and take a place of equality.

The world that we call Mother,
holds the space for what the ego or the soul needs to create,
and gives a stage for you to search for your light.

The dark you live in will only keep you in walls,
encasing yourself in that which exists in your mind
and the poisons you consume each day.

To slip in your disgrace, and only for you,
for the words you say to become true.
You must watch your tongue and the taste of venom,
as they will only engage with a past version of you.

Unconscious Conspiracy

Demon of the past,
stay in your cave of torment,
keep tearing yourself in two.
This was your choice.

The words that you speak,
have become spells that keep you incomplete.
So, stop the disgust,
It's making your soul rust.

As it hardens in each segment,
your soul has been delivered to the dark shadows
that keep you captive in sin.

As we are protected from your unconscious conspiracy.
We are light,
and live with the sun in our soul
in every life and story told.

We aren't sold so easily, to the voices of venom that destroyed your heart.
So, keep in your cave until you finally split in two.

Sleepwalking Reality

Covering your mouth isn't the only mask society has placed on us,
life can be an ever-endless sleepwalking existence.
The skin of an impure aesthetic withers the soul.

To portray yourself in a light that isn't from Source's story
strips you of your divinity and destined frequency.

Wear you with pride,
tear at the show you try to make,
as this is your spirit killer,
the one that makes u feel the distrust.

The escape you try to walk through
is a time warp of a never-ending purgatory
that stops the access to one's pure reality.

The real,
the love,
the vibe.

Even when you think are alone you will never truly be,
as you have a will of integrity.
So, stop the fake and take back your real identity.

Heartbreak Isn't Yours

The heartbreak isn't yours,
it's the torment of another that will never be able to feel love,
as the self-loathing has destroyed the soul's sweet side.

Others have seen through the lies that you told so many times
that they have created a life of never-ending escapism.

To walk alone, even when surrounded with others as the former sleepwalks.
A distraction that weakens the one that was meant for so much more.

So, don't sit with what you must not heal,
but allow the gifts they left that created such a beautiful whole.

Poisoned Pleasure

The lingering taste of a past that created a puppet of poisoned pleasure,
to be used and played with,
even though the soul's fire was fading.

The lies and secrets became a feast,
a gate to where the purest one became addicted to pain.

To find only happiness in a space of hell
became easier than to lose a connection
to a ghost who dies to be loved.

To give each and every piece has been the demise,
yet in our time shared you became a brighter being,
this was when it was the last let go.

No more a prisoner of a purgatory of pleasing,
but a person of peace and purpose,
has emerged out of the fire of dark desire.

Won't Ever Lie

Want to know a story?
It might scare you,
it might make you cry,
but it won't ever lie.
So, sit down and make some space.

It's time to listen to the story.
Of the one where you have already lived,
a life that has been perfect in every moment.

Each segment leads to a creation of the inner manifesto
which man had held the power to for an eternity.

The chapters are finally coming together.
The beginning of a fairytale,
where the hero had to come to save the heart of happiness.

From the monsters, to the dangerous settings the past portrayed,
the end is where the yin entered
to rebalance the years of the yang state.

So, no more turning the pages quickly to get to the end,
take pleasure in devouring each word.

Dusk Begins

The two sides of me that yearn for the total opposite.
I try to hide the endless temptation to creep into the seductive soul.

The noir night that ignites a character of corruption,
creates so much pleasure in sweet pain that it can't be denied.

For if all was light, it would never be noticed.
The dusk begins, and the temptress starts to cast her creation of indulgence.

A taste of escapism in the spirits allow the others in the vessel
to release the angelic
to begin the night of dark desire.

Still when the amalgamation of mischief takes over
and fills the deepest belly of indecent temptation,
the black sky transforms as the sun comes up
to return the depraved to dust.

Shadow Side

Taking all my words away was a crime that took your soul away.
As you creep further into the dark of the night with two-sided friends,
you lose the gifts of the mother.

The pleas of a family that saw the change of a Narcissus in love with his shadow,
which slowly became his demise.

So as your tongue twists in its snake form,
you realise that you're not as clever as your reptilian curse is telling you.

As you are incapable of love,
only pleasure for an inner world,
which wrought such self-insulation,
that your web of entrust started to twist you as its prey.

The roles have changed for eternity.
So, slither back to your cage with the monsters you let
devour more of your soul day by day.

Storm of Lies

When you live in the eye of the storm, a peace like no other can be found.
For the fight to get there has been a whirlwind your life had no control of.

Tearing at the ego and skin
that society wanted to place you in,
has been an illusion that your real reality tore away.

As when you have felt the most powerful elements,
like the wind of sheer worry,
a tornado of threats
and a hurricane of hurt,
you can sit with the clarity that even in the middle of this,
it won't purvey any pain.

So, sit in your own perfect storm of lies,
love lost
and a life you thought you wanted,
before you see the clear skies of your time.

Dark Meditation

Sometimes what we see, isn't what is real. We have an inner dialogue that can tilt our reality, alongside residual shadows on the mind, which we sometimes need to ground ourselves with before finding our authentic vision.

This heat breathwork is to connect your inner vision with the warmth of your breath and body, to find an inner stillness and tranquillity of your own divine individual beauty.

To begin, you should find yourself a quiet space where you won't get disturbed, so you can settle into your Light Work breathing practice.
Next find how your body wants to adhere to this breath work.
Do you have a lot of energy? If so, would it be better to stand in a tree pose? Or a neutral position? Perhaps sat down, cross legged on the floor? Or if you desire a true timeout, lay down in a Shavasana pose with closed eyes or a soft stare.

After you have sought comfort for your body, connect with your natural breath. Observe how it fills your belly with life giving energy and how you expel the warmth your body has created. This warmth is what we are going to connect with for the next part of the practice.

After 20 natural inhales and exhales, you are going to start rubbing your hands with vigour for around 30 seconds. This is to create heat. When you feel the intense heat of the friction your hands have created, you are going to place them over your eyes. Feel the heat penetrate the eyes and enjoy the feeling of the senses you are receiving. Now think of all the gifts you receive with your sight every day, like cloud formations, a smile of a stranger, or the green of nature.

You can repeat this section 4 times, connecting with your gratitude for the abundance of visuals you receive. This practice, when done frequently, can connect warmth with gratitude, a feeling which is a gift that the living often receive without appreciation.

We need to connect with our own individual beauty, not that which society has determined. You are beautiful. Remember this each time you do the dark meditation in order to connect with the warmth of the practice.

Now return to your natural rhythmic breathing for the desired amount of time. When you come out of this state, take in the colours and visuals, be present and accept the light. As even in the dark, the warmth of the light can be found.

Element Eight

Light.

"If you light a lamp for someone else, it will also brighten your path"

Buddha

Stars Can Shine Brighter

The bits you don't like in me are the only invitation to find you,
as we are one,
and when we feel resistance, work has to be done.

Your inner world only shouts out to the external what you're really about.
So, if you shine, the stars can shine brighter.

Don't hide in the dark.
Find your network of those who find their soul's bliss in song, word, and art.
For this is what makes us different.

We are the gift,
the presence of a difference.
Don't let it get wrapped up in society's dilution of the energetic few.
Baby just be you.

Let the Fruits Flourish

I am not the captive,
you are not the hunter.
Can we go back to when we were like brother and sister?

Friends that made no sense to each other,
in a world we were only beginning to step into,
both so vulnerable and young.

The story can still be changed,
you don't have to be chained to the poison that runs through your veins.

Return to the boy that dreamt,
and drew magic in his pages,
which sadly turned into rages,
that tore down the little girl he used to love.

So, let's pretend it never happened and start anew.
Now there is more than just you.
The fruits of a seasonal love are yet to flourish again.

So, grow and branch out as much as possible.
So, the kin have something to hold onto.

Boy with a Bear's Courage

It's the tale of a boy who held a queen's heart.
For when she forgot who she was, his love was the only cure.

With messages of 'I love you' and 'Care for the kin',
this boy with a bear's courage held on from when it began.

To hold each other in an eternity,
is the love that is true -
a love of a son and his mother.
Thank you for being you.

For never giving up on life, that is beautiful like a piece of art.
Oh darling, you really touched my heart.

No Clone of Society

Stop running away from who you are,
hiding your true beauty has always been your demise.

The cloud of society will never know what it takes to be really unique:
an endless under current of internal conversations.

The rhythmic waves of a rhapsody of revolving revelations
releases the soul into the light.

No more pushing, allow your story to unfold,
like the lotus revealing the soul to the light.

Love, connection, friendship and time are so pure and beautiful,
their radiance could make you cry.

You are through the dirt and are beautiful
in your own unique complicated crushed creativity.

In the Arms of Mother

To hear the story of who you used to be
is a most terrifying story that just doesn't seem real anymore.

The lies and programming of a past of victimisation
has been raised to a crescendo, that broke every part of you.

A soul that had to be rebirthed in the arms of Mother Gaia.
A mother herself, bathed in a baptism of brilliance, she finally accepted.

To rest is ok, now that you have made your fairytale out of nightmares,
yet Karma is here to reside now, so sleep well little Starshine.

Thin Thread of Time

A thin thread of time.
This is all it will be,
where the uncomfortable became the love of self.

To find one's inner through the views of others, can never be true.
As there are many thousands of versions of you.

So be sure of who you want to be,
listen and speak with integrity,
you are awake, whilst the others sleep.

So, keep on moving through your thread in time
and stir the others in pure divine,
as to sing and laugh is just enough.

Time to wave the others off, on tides of space that waste no love,
for consciousness is upon us, my dear love.

Beat of a Butterfly

The heart space begins to flutter,
like the first beat of the butterfly's wings.
The change has happened from a life of struggle
encased in fear.

The dangers were real,
yet the fears only existed in a cocoon of manmade externals,
that penetrated the environment of the beginning.

The hard bits have evolved from the tight binding of one's true authenticity.
In the skin of struggle, the only way to let go is to surrender.

To be seen to escape the constricting space you made.
Nevertheless, it was so important for this momentum of magic to happen.

So spread the wings of your heart and find your other beautiful blessed,
to see the world as a new soul that you have always been.

Set the Future Free

The fragility of love's trust is one that can cause
questions of past mind traps,
that were set to destroy the innocent.

For we must remember to be like a feather in the wind,
which has no direction yet still has the trust in its flight.

For when we fly, we can play in the pleasures of the present, that the past
cannot disturb.
You can now rest by allowing yourself to let go.

You must surrender to the feeling of trust,
just because the other loves have rusted
don't let this be discussed.

For now, you are free to flow in the winds of enchantment,
to find your golden wings that set the future free.

Layers of Lies

It's how we get to the gifts which is the real story.
From a past of puppeteering you created a phoenix who was always ready to fly.

When we feel safe is the only time we can open the gates to recover
and reassure the relationship with self.

To live in a life laced with layers of lies was always going to cause rot.
As when something has been created in hate,
the opposite you should always anticipate.

It will grow and flourish under the deep dirt
that has spilled from a soul of dark sorcery
because the illusions were never real.

As the years passed, the spirit that once was lost and blindfolded,
found the way with the magic of nature, Source, and self.

The dark will never remain,
as even on the blackest of nights,
if we really look,
we can see the brightest of stars.

Heart to Heart Space

Your place is here sweet child,
heart to heart space generating a love so pure
that it creates new worlds of manifestation.

Magic moving within my vessel, as one touch can never be enough.
The heat, taste and energy can never be replaced.

A relationship that heals every time we connect.
As this is the only time we have, that will be so painfully missed.

So, lie with me and make me more,
in the only way you can.

Just Because

Just because you want me, doesn't mean it's enough.
I wasted my tears,
that became so many fears,
of the promises you wasted.

No more going back for my soul to be crushed
and my inner voice never to be heard.

It can never be the best bits,
never just be easy.
For this is the fickle fairytale you created,
so, you could allow your beast to slumber.

Yet still the guarded gates have been entered
and the princess has been saved by the purest of love's passions,
a peace and protection so sweet.

Light Meditation

The Light Work meditation is one of recharging and reconnecting to Mother Earth, as well as the Universe. We get nourishment from our food, relationships and environments. Yet nature and the sun still charge our cells to bring additional love to our spirits in the most natural way.

For this exercise you will need to wait for a dry day, when the Sun is shining. You can sit on a park bench, cross-legged on the ground, or stand in your garden or even at a window, to receive the magic healing rays. Once you have found your chosen place, direct yourself to the sun and make sure your eyes are closed. Make sure you maintain good physical form, if sat down your palms should face upwards and your spine should be neutral.

Now loosen your shoulders by pulling them down, start to unfurrow your brow and release your jaw. Relax, it's time to be at peace. With your relaxed face, closed eyes and sun facing you, start to feel the beautiful heat and light that assists this world to grow, connect with this growth and just be. Breathe easy, don't overthink, just feel, be, receive and love the moment you are at one with.

Be still in this moment, feel the sun's energy penetrating your skin and nurturing the cells with the precious vitamin D you need to thrive. Your arms should be visible and your legs too, if possible, and sit or stand for up to 15 minutes. If the sun is intense, switch to your other side so that you're not directly facing the sunlight.

You only get one vessel and to honour it is a blessing. So give light to your soul and as you charge, remember the sun will always be out to heal and help you shine – as it is one of nature's purest designs.

Element Nine

Trust.

"Life will give you whatever experience is most helpful for the evolution of your consciousness. How do you know this is the experience you need? Because this is the experience you are having at the moment"

Eckhart Tolle.

The Tribe as One

Only when you lose the structure
of a mankind that hides behind so many masks,
can you truly see yourself.

Hear the beat of the Earth,
the drum of the deep voice of who you truly are,
and the species of what we feel inside.

For some are from stars,
some are from the oceans,
and the plains of other planets.
So, when we search for our real history,
this is when the divine will shine.

The energetic being that you are,
that moves in emotions to restore
the layers of the true new world order.

Rise, rip the skin of the system
and surrender.
Only then will the tribe be as one,
to be invited to the connection of Source.

Through song,
prayer,
breath,
words,
nature,
dance with all of the pleasures
that should be free,
these are humanity's treasures
that find us all.

This Love Was Never Yours

Take your time
across the line,
In never ending moments
that twist and turn with strength
will be the constant reminders.

That love you lost
was never yours.
All the thoughts of glory,
it's time to take your time
and take that next turning.

As in this constant roundabout
you will access only yearning,
for the destination can't be yours,
just don't stop learning.

Don't look back,
just keep on sunshine girl you're smiling.
So, take a break and find a love -
the one that has always been driving to you.
For Source is here,
she will navigate you well into the world,
serving first,
as this is when we are as one.

For when we do this,
this is when it's all done for love,
so, keep moving on.

By the Sister's Hand

Weighed down,
way down.
Don't let that inner ego take you down,
As that's all down to mother nature.

Celebrate her,
it's our way out.
Stray to get to the connected
and go down,
hear your internal spirit speak wisdom.

Keep on going way down,
take your souls sister by the hand
and hold on tight,
just keep on going all the way out.

Luna Love

Moon goddess,
your movement through the sky collides with clear consciousness,
you are the one that is surrounded by stars.

For you light up the sky
and are a blessing to the space
that you create.

Moving through your phases
with grace and enchantment,
your planetary magic
is a manifestation of pure courage.

For you will always be there
to light the way,
even in the mistiest nights.
Your purpose of luna love
is clearing the way.

The Golden Elements

As we walk on the path,
that is layered with years of mistrust
and the dust of past dismay,
each step we go over
will cause the magic to appear.

Step by step,
the layers will fade away,
and the golden elements of your Source
will start to shine through.

Like when we walk through the leaves
and the sunshine catches our faces.
The rays of joy that heaven sent
will uncover the truth,
the beauty that will always repair.

So, keep the quest strong and clear,
stay blessed on your way through the trails of trust,
to find your guide you must.

Freak Release

Freak release to unfold
the new abilities that you never told.
For now, we move into the next dimension.

Free from the ego
and the power of the inhumane,
The spirit is all that exists
and is older than time.

For the ether feels
that you're deeply divine
with the love of your authenticity -
which will always win,
so just keep breathing in.

Release the core of the lives of lies,
exhale the society that dictates,
and dive into the ocean of you,
drowning in the acceptance of time,
patience
and a love so true.

Entangle into a World

Breath in,
hold it
and escape.
For the space that you now find,
is where your growth can start.

Do you remember,
all the wonderful things
that you asked for life to bring?
So, sit in the knowledge
that your souls divine is coming
at the perfect time.

To love and entangle into a world that most won't find,
for the love of the spirits
is difficult to find.

A deeper connection,
that only few possess,
and can bring a feeling of shy regress.

However, this is your gift dear spirit child,
You know it's already been written
so take your vow and live in pure bliss.

Space Voyager

The lake is deep dear space voyager,
with each ripple you lay upon,
another will seek
and call out for your movement.

The unrest is unsettling
and when you float
on that echoing odyssey sky,
dare to dream your life complete.

The moons of old can make
your spell of wonder and magic come true,
for your secret is safe with the skies.
The stars reveal the path of virtue
to the realm your heart is searching for,
of pure compassion, love and understanding.

Earth travelling in this moment
and your friend is soon to come to meet in this world,
as you have lived on the other planets that are now in ruins.

Castles in the Sky

As the moon drips over me,
I have to remember,
that all the dreams that can take me to sadness
will always be gone as the sun rises,

Every day is a new blessing,
where the conscious dream
can become reality's connection
with your inner child.

Play your days away,
with pride and purity for when we were young
and all could be done on a daily basis.

So, take your castles
that you build in the clouds
and let the solar light shine through
as sure as the sky is blue,
stay true.

Acorns of Hope

The passing of time will find the love you were truly born to make,
the passage into the realm of humanity has had its curses,
escape into the other dimensions,
your soul will still be heard.

To listen is the hardest thing,
and to talk is the internal dialogue
that mankind has programmed into your vessel.

So like the big old oak,
trust that your acorns of hope
will come good
to start the journey of growth.

There are many branches,
and some will snap,
some will rot.
Nevertheless,
the roots will secure you with the support of mother nature.

So,
trust the ups,
the downs,
the inside outs,
the twists and turns,
they only ground you.

The Angel Meditation

Trusting in yourself can be overwhelming at times, but it doesn't have to be, for you are always surrounded with love and light. The angels have been sent down to support your divine being and this is what you have to put your trust in. The angels have supported me in all areas of my life, and this is my appreciation of their love for us all. Angels are the protectors and guides of our lives' purposes; all you have to do is ask and trust that the Archangels are guiding you in the right direction - even when it doesn't feel like it! Remember, the light is always here; even in darkness you look up and the moon and stars will light the way for your soul.

The Angel Meditation is a calling to the Archangel Raphael: the angel of healing who uses his green light to heal. Archangel Raphael is the angel of the spirits of man, and it is his duty to heal the Earth. He is recognised by both Saints in the East and the West. Raphael means 'he who heals', or 'God heals. He wants to relieve your stress and comfort you by healing any personal ailments that you may be suffering from. As a Reiki Healer I work with angels via their guidance to heal. Through this book I've been brought to connect you with the Archangel Raphael.

Trust in the love and healing you are about to access, this meditation is simple and can be done by laying down in a Shavasana pose: sat cross-legged on the floor or upright in a chair, the spine should be in a neutral yet aligned position and you should be comfortable in order to access your peace. In your chosen position, close your eyes and breath in through your nose, feeling the cold air being inhaled, and now exhale the warm air. Find an organic breathwork pattern and in your mind repeat these lines with love and power:

> "I call upon and put my trust in Archangel Raphael. Thank you for sending your energetic healing into my vessel to aid my journey of self-love and compassion." – repeat this five times.

Now return to your organic breath flow for the rest of your meditation, this can be anywhere from 5 to 30 minutes.
Trust that love and healing is all around you. Thank you, Archangel Raphael.

Element Ten

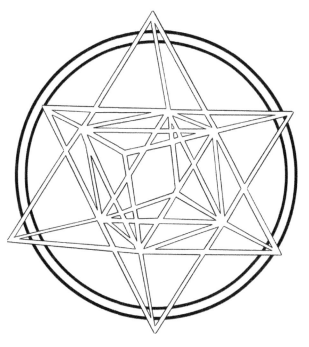

Purity.

"Purity or impurity depends on oneself,
no one can purify another"

Gautama Buddha.

Faith's Storm

For the respect must be given.
The prayers must be said.
Angelic love has got to be spread.

For the ones that don't have a voice are truly masked.
They are the ones that live with an unsettling task.

So, we will be the ones to shine.
To shine so hard it transmutes through time,
into love and compassion for other sides.

The angels are here for you,
in energy and physical form.
So, trust in good,
and release into Faith's storm.

This is the only way we can repay.
To pay for a life that has been stolen away.

We have been blessed,
where many others have only been suppressed.
Missing from birth in such a way,
or taken away into a world of dark and dismay.

So, light a candle.
Say some words.
But don't forget,
the strength of love will always be heard.

This is for the children, the women, the blood, the sweet souls taken.
Justice is coming through the power of love.

Keep on healing through this space and time,
as all are connected,

so please make haste.

Thank you, truth tellers,
keep shining your lights.
This is our new world
and they will be loved with all of God's might.

--For Human Trafficking Awareness--

A Petal to Complete.

For the chill comes from deep within,
the guilt of seeds that others have planted,
yet dear one you must still remember,
you're complete.

You are the one who tends to the watering,
the nurturing,
the growth.
Sometimes the seed needs time.

For weeds still have flowers
and beauty deep;
wisdom in magic
that can heal deep relief.

Don't stop the seed from the life it was given,
but change your words,
the vibe,
the rhythm,
for you are always what you were meant to be.

A rose in the thorns,
Is sometimes incomplete,
but with the sun,
the rain and Earth so deep,
you can always grow a petal
and become unearthed.

The Crown and the Ego

Love and touch,
your heart desires,
but your mind says no.
Why is it so hard to let you go?

The tales that won't come true,
as the king has lost his throne of protection
and the ego knows.

As the maiden calls out for devotion,
the ego denies the notion,
as this life has lived lifetimes through the stars.

This Earth angel will not give in,
for the missing is her quest
and her ego is lost.
She won't give up on the tests for the crown.

So, sweet Light Maiden don't be scared,
your healing will come
and you will wear your gown of starlight
on love's throne.

Time to Waste

Time is the only thing we have,
time to discover our true authenticity,
time to waste a little,
whilst we patiently see what will be.

This lifetime is like the clouds passing through the sky:
a fleeting moment like the sunrise.

That is why our time is precious,
don't let it set too soon sunshine soul;
keep changing,
keep rising
and take your own sweet time.

The Way that we Be

Your love and respect
are all that you have,
so treat others
as you would like to be treated.

No regrets,
just take the time
and really see,
there is a lot in this world
that we need to be.

Strong,
courageous,
true
and honest -
the way we live is the way we be.

So be the one that fights for the right, do the honourable thing
and don't turn out the light.

Just flow the love through your field
and make the difference for real, because everyone is waking up.

Desert Dissent

In her divine time,
she will make you want to stay,
for her respect of Source,
is a strong passageway.

Her mind and her body,
a vessel of love,
that spills over,
into the sky above.

A connection so pure
she could bring you to tears,
this goddess of strength
will be with me for years.

A woman of trust
and pure belief,
her story is unique.

A desert traveller
of clear intent,
I thank you soul sister
for this dissent.

Secret Garden of Desire

Back to the secret garden of desires,
where the wildflowers are enthralled with thorns
and weave their way to the sky.

Swaying in the breeze,
a melancholy mix of raw emotions,
from desire to solitude.

The flowers of peace,
growing and pollenating
protection and purity,
whilst the dried dead ones that once encapsulated so much beauty,
have wasted away.

The desire to be more beautiful and bolder have the lessons untold.
The practice of just being
is the magic - to sway in the wind
and love what we are.

From the daisy to the dandelion,
we are just enough.

Lived this Life Before

Don't be scared of the unknown,
you know it more than you will ever know,
for you have lived this life before.

The fear is just your shield,
so be brave and yield,
know your worth and be the flow
of ever endlessly letting go.

You are your guide,
don't overthink your body and soul, know your role:
you are loved and accepted.

Don't look back and hesitate,
wrap in those many layers of connection,
as dear Source you are so wise,
so please let it go
and enjoy this time.

Be like the Mist

As the mist makes it way over
the mornings that grow darker,
remember this is only time,
and it will pass.

Look for the beauty in the unworthy,
as there is always a layer of love wrapped in the mistrust.

Sometimes people don't know how to love,
the teachers didn't learn the language
and the lessons were never put in place.

Don't let this take away your true nature,
don't lose that child you once were,
that loved and laughed with eternal trust,
that forgave in a heartbeat
and never judged.

Be like the mist and transcend over the morning for you are awake.

The Mother Lost

As she looks up to the sky,
it will turn from the grey
that blurred her vision,
and made the lies seem so real.

The rain falls under her eyes,
and she cries for the girl that the mother lost,
the pain is its own blessing.

From the torture,
the therapy begins to take its time,
cell by cell,
to unchain the maiden of mother medicines.

The Earth calls to all the lost,
that now know it's their time to be found
by the others who yearn to love.

Love each other in soul and spirit;
connect, for the foes have been forgotten
and the miracles have been revealed.

Counting Meditation

To find a piece of calm in modern day society can be so hard, partly because the external has migrated into the inner mind and to even try to find space to think can be overwhelming sometimes. That's why this simple counting meditation is the Light Work practice of Element 7: Purity. This is a brilliant way to start meditating if you have never tried it before, as it can help keep you grounded with a simple technique.

To begin, you want to find a quiet place where you won't get disturbed, where it is peaceful and comfortable; you could choose to sit in a chair with your spine in a neutral position and the crown of your head facing up to receive from the Universe, or cross-legged on the floor, or even lying down in a relaxed Shavasana pose. One cannot experience purity in an overtly stimulating environment; overactive thought patterns and actions don't serve your higher self.

Relax your shoulders, loosen your brow and soften your jaw. For your first inhalation, take a deep breath in for a count of four. Now hold for a count of four and exhale to the count of eight. Repeat this first counting cycle for four rounds.

Now you want to start counting each breath. Inhale as one, exhale as two, inhale as three and so on, until you reach ten. Once you have reached ten, return to one. This is simple but the process keeps the brain on track so you can relax. If you find yourself wondering off in your thoughts, don't worry - just start at one again.

Do this until you have meditated for your desired length of time (this can be 5-30 minutes). When coming around from this meditation, slowly wiggle the toes and fingers, rotate the wrists and open your eyes, give yourself adequate time to recalibrate to your external surroundings and note the difference. You could reflect on what your mind was feeling like prior to the counting meditation, and what it is feeling like now. This timeout is necessary to connect to a purer path of thoughts and feelings, so whenever you get lost, remember, it's as easy as counting to ten, taking a deep breath and coming back to the moment.

Element Eleven

Connection.

"What you seek is seeking you"

Rumi

Letting Me Let It Go

The boy who was once my hero
and who had always held a place
for as long as this tale has been in full grace.

The man who has the heart of a lion,
And a pride of friends that always seek him,
his words are wise
and roar into the souls that need to hear.

With loyal language and an ever-creative mind,
to access other places of magician's rapture.
The spirit, like the elegant hummingbird, is called to the sweet flower.

For the friends who live in their separate worlds of abstract,
create clarity in reality.
What is real in this world?
We will never know.

Just the times of purity,
connection and being able to let go.
Thank you, dear hero,
thanks for letting me let it go.

Mist of Mystery

The mist has the mystery,
the secrets of the ego.
When you walk and can't see your true reality any longer,
is when the goddess of the mist will clear your visions.

The vision of the heart that can't let go,
another loss of trust and connection.

The mind that has become too busy
with the lies and noncommitment.

The body that is released into its unique vigor,
which is no longer the slave of seduction.

The goddess of the clouds invites you to walk with her,
so, the mist will cleanse your soul,
allow the wind to strip you bare;
for only then you will feel at ease.

Surrender the past and take the next step into your loves lost.
Walk in ecstasy and rapture,
as dear soul spirit the magic has been awakened.

Another of nature's guides has worked her medicine
for you to go on your soul mission.
So, when you feel lost, go deeper to the point you can't see,
the point of fear - face it to become all you can be.

Lie with This Love

A love that has waited a lifetime.
Where have you been my dear?
To hear you now, and without fear, feels so sincere.

To lie with this love, in complete utter trust,
has changed our lives forever.
I know we will shine together, in all weathers.

To walk with each other,
and hear every unspoken word of magic intertwine
was the love of a quest, of the pure divine.

For I will go forever,
chasing this piece of time -
even if the world was in decline.
This will be a love of everlasting design.

Together We are Home

Together we are home.
For a place of love is the mortar of how we shine,
the family of souls that never stop learning.

Always returning to ground in their individual ways,
nevertheless, always together.

A family of trust and eternal support,
an infinity of love that can never be disputed,
as the allowing of self has always been the key.

As the elders have passed their lessons,
it is now time for the kin,
the ones that went a little further with the wings of family,
guiding the flight to new beginnings.

So never feel alone,
always feel loved,
because we have us.

Play of Pleasures

Pain, pain, go away
maybe come back another day.

Even though you may want to stay still,
it's not time to play.
New friends have been made,
there's no more space for this cliché.

The playground of torment and teasing is over,
the new game is not to pretend,
but dream in every waking moment.

Your soul mates have come to align with a play of pleasures and practices,
that make a lifetime of magic.

Thankful for the bullies of past,
as this was the awakening a soul needed
from the first lesson of life.

So, dance, sing, write to your soul's content dear inner child.
Your memories of not fitting in are finally finding their place,
in your enchanted jigsaw of self-expression.

Finding You

In finding you,
I found myself a compassionate connection
of love and affection.

To have the security of Source,
is a secret I'm so glad you didn't keep.

It is the key to our lock,
love lives here.

Love is in our room,
love is our moment
and love is us.

I am love,
you are love
and we are love.

Let the organic growth of petals of passion
lace our souls together.

A new world has been created
with a conscious creativity like no other.

For you are me,
and I am you,
and this is love.

Quest for a Soul

Putting me back together,
piece by piece,
was never going to be easy.

The heart that broke and hid itself in the galaxies,
the quest for a soul that wasn't afraid to get lost.

The flame that searches on the tail of a shooting star
to find a smile,
a brave dive into a blackhole
to scrape back a little of her soul.

A spaceman has learnt the lesson of loneliness,
so isn't afraid to look for the heart's treasure,
even if it takes a lifetime.

So, keep going rocket man, collect your tears of diamond aura,
tension that could tear a planet in two.
This will be the passion,
which searches for you.

A Lion's Heart

A lion's heart with a roar so loud that it will only ever be heard.
But in truth: a courageous cub full of mischief and bravery.
Sweet boy don't change.

You can't choose to take away the pride you have been gifted with.
The confidence of your control is so strong,
even when you're so young.

You have been sent here to prowl in protection for a lifetime,
keeping your sweet loved kin safe.

But remember we don't always have to align,
as long as we have each other we have the faith that we can survive any famine.

For you are here to lead little love.
Just allow yourself to be playful first,
the thirst of your elder can wait.
Remember you are free.

Feathers Come Together

The little bird who sings every day,
she is so beautiful in every way.
A feather of empathy to love like no other,
a feather of trust that has become her heart's tether.

This bird thought she was flying free,
but she wasn't all she could be -
as the cage of confinement started to tighten.

Accessing the places she could feel free began to frighten,
as the flight of imagination started to tear.
Tear at her emotion.

She knew the words she needed to speak,
to finally make herself complete,
but still the little bird was caught in the trap.
A trap that man feeds to dull the songstress's soul.

So dear beauty don't give up now.
As you are the key, there is no doubt.

So, fly with your feathers of true integrity;
your life is waiting,
you only have to turn the key.

The World Stands Still

While the world stands still,
our love is so powerful that is passes through every paradigm of time.

For you are my angel, meant to partner with me
as this is a connection of pure integrity.

The flame of a love that broke us in two
So that each other's dreams could come true,
is the only manifestation that helped me hold onto you.

So, keep on living and letting go
because Bby we are the awakened –
that old life died years ago.

Thank God for helping me lead me to you.

Residue of the Mind

To have loved in past, doesn't take away the moments you make today.
The love that previously took that space can only evaporate,
or cause a condensation of unconsciousness,
that when wiped away will heal a residue of the mind.

The process of letting go, letting out and living in the now,
was a lesson the inner child had to wait for
to really play with the passions it was keeping secret.

For when we shine in real time, the present will become the gift:
the gift of love, laughter and a life without any strife.

So, step into the minutes that you create with confidence
and trust that the dust of the old ego
has been blown away with the sweet past.

Connection Meditation

This rebalancing Light Work meditation is for the times when we feel a little disconnected. Life in the modern day, where anything can be sprung on us at any moment and life can change like the flip of a coin, can sometimes be detrimental to our overall well-being. This Connection Light Work breathing exercise helps with balancing the cognitive, slowing down the physical demands of life and connecting to the soul to be able to clarify and feel gratitude for the Source and love that we have all been placed on Mother Earth to experience.

Firstly, you should try to find a relaxing space where you can give yourself the required time to fulfil a practice of grounding and equalising your body's homeostasis. When you have aligned with the space, it is time to get comfortable for your practice; so either standing in a neutral position with a straight spine so that your crown chakra is aligned to receive the universal love, sat down, or even in a laying down posture like a Shavasana or Butterfly pose (in which the soles of the feet are pressed together and the knees open up to touch the floor on either side) – a great exercise which can release tightness around the hips.

Relax your shoulders, unfurrow your brow and soften your jaw. When you are comfortable with your pose for this Connection breathwork, you should start with a deep, full breath into the belly and the lungs for 4 seconds. Hold this for 4 seconds. Now a long exhale for 8 seconds. Now repeat this breathing cycle three more times in order to sink into a rhythmic breathwork.

The next step is to place the thumb of your left hand over your left nostril, your two middle fingers are going to be straight and placed on the brow/third eye and the ring finger will be placed over to the right, just hovering so you can still inhale before we begin.

To start, we lift the left finger off the nostril, while the right is holding the other nostril down, so that we can concentrate on breathing entirely through our left nasal passage. Inhale for a count of 4. Hold for 4. Now close the left nasal passage and exhale for a count of 6-8 out of the right nasal passage exclusively.

Now we do the same thing but with the other nostril, lifting the right finger off of the nostril whilst the left is held down. Concentrate on breathing entirely through your right nostril. You can extend this for 10 rounds in total.

After you have completed your ten rounds of your connection breathwork, you are going to return to your natural breathing rhythm. This can be up to 5-30 minutes depending on the amount of time you have or how you are feeling.

When you have decided that you feel ready to return, have a little think about how your body feels. Is it less tense? Is your head clearer? Do you feel more relaxed?

Keep connected and when you feel out of alignment, just remember you can sit by yourself at any time to re-connect.

Element Twelve

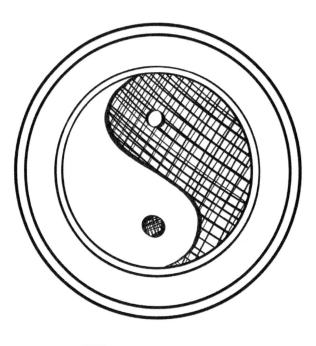

Love.

"You yourself, as much as anybody in the Universe, deserve your love and affection"

Mahatama Gandhi.

Hues of Heaven

Love yourself baby,
you only got one shot at this,
be the woman you were born to be.

The one that creates her own frequency,
full on power.
But still remember,
past the thorns lies a delicate rose.

The daily water is necessary,
the most beautiful secret garden that blooms
will set eyes alight with all its glory,
yet only when the keeper unlocks the gate,
to nourish her with love's story.

When the keeper grows lazy,
the vibrancy starts to fade-out.
Not visible day by day,
still in time the hues of heaven became dull.

Some life had given up,
but the channels of roots never gave up.
Even when the flowers bloomed without radiance,
that garden always believed.

Dear rose,
don't forget you will always grow,
but take care of your secret garden with diligence and duty

For you don't have to be a secret anymore,
open the gates to your fields of flowers
that show their pure,
unique and unfolding love.

Treasured City

Like that extra ten minutes of snoozing,
which feels so good despite the regret.
It's how you start the passage
that sets the tone for the journey.

There will be trips that mark the skin and sting on the path of your body,
nevertheless each scar has its own unique story.

From past loves,
detachment,
support and self-acceptance,
don't look too deep as your elegance starts within the veneer of your life.

So, dance with the breeze
and keep on your yellow brick road baby girl,
the next turn is only ahead
and it's your treasured city.

Take your time and wait for the three clicks,
the whirlwind will settle
and you will sparkle with the ones you love,
the real gems -
the ones who really steal the show.

Rolling Away in Dreams

I'm only going for that zing baby.
When are you going to see
that this isn't a want it's a need,
the way you make me feel?

Let's go deep into the rhapsody of rhythm,
from the limbs that link
with electricity that enlightenments them when they begin.

Losing ourselves in past passions,
from dusk till the dawn
they warm each other's souls within.

There won't be more mourning
as the sacramental ceremony begins
and the twin flames dance in the darkness,
only seeing each other.

Rolling away into dreams that are so real
that they can feel them.
The whisper from another year
sings from lips so sincere.

That soul mate fire that only few taste
is mighty,
don't make such haste,
just wait
and sit knowing this love will be embraced.

Friends in a Minute

Why does this have to stop?
This childlike connection
where we can be friends in one minute
and always have the power to make up after a breakup,
again and again.

Why does that inner child have to grow up?
Why can't we always create a love that comes from fun and play?

Age is irrelevant
and connection is everything.
So, dear inner child
I allow you once again to rise from birth to this day.
I pass thanks inner child
for everything I ever wanted to know.

I Am Enough

I am enough,
I am enough.
The right amount of joy,
I am of me
to give abundantly.

Sometimes it is time to say enough,
It is enough
to love your mind,
body and soul.

It is time to say I've had enough,
to stop the beliefs of others
that keep you tied to an old way of living.

The new world has arrived,
and you are enough,
enough to experience you,
in pure compassion and acceptance.

For the soul of your old story has been tough.
This has been the prophecy of enough.

Dear Lotus

Be
The vibe,
The energy,
The purpose
In your life.

Create the dream and live bright, because dear lotus this is your life.

This is the life you were given,
so, stand up,
be sprite,
be bold
and sometimes be told.

Because this is your dance
and your spirit cannot be sold

So,
be
The vibe
The energy
The purpose
This is your life.

Mirror Maiden

To the one that will always understand the mirror maiden in my life.

A heart so beautiful it touches everyone she meets,
as she takes her time with pride
and peace.

Her elegance will capture your heart, it's the kind of magic that can spellbind
souls.

To this goddess in my life,
I thank you sweet girl for all you are, for making dreams feel so real
and comforting the lonely nights.

Keep capturing the love
in every way you do
because a vision like you
can never be doubted.

2 Sons of a Daughter, My Kings

The two sons of a daughter,
who's souls of golden light
dance on the sands of crystal charm.

The sonshines that choose me
to weave their magic of mischief
and mesmerise the mother's spirit.

As each warms the heart,
the boys grow into their future tales
to fill the mother's life with glory.

Though the time will slip away,
the connection will never fade,
two boys and the forever story of love.

Segment in Time

For the weeks are only days,
and as each moment passes,
the time comes closer.

Nevertheless,
enjoy all the moments in-between growth,
feel and love
through each segment of time

With the sea air on your skin
and the sun shining into your blessed soul,
take care as each wave comes.

For today is all we have,
so keep on sailing through,
as the stars light up the night,
so all your wishes can come true.

Waves of Worlds

Into a voyage of unknown excitement,
for the turbulent times have been and gone.

The light is always there
for you to know the passage,
just allow the waves of worlds below.

As the elements mix and co-create,
the balance will begin through one,
the lover's warmth will let you know of the beauty held within.

For the one who moves with tides can open the hearts of others,
to keep the flames without fuel,
hold fierce.

So, wish them well,
the ones who dared to sail
on an ocean of stars that light
the body,
the heart,
the mind
and move into each other's soul.

Words of Compassion Practice

Compassion is one of the keys to successful self-love and the love of others. To feel for ourselves as we do for others, is one of the most important lessons of life that we all will learn on our paths to a higher self. Like the Dalai Lama explains in his book 'The Art of Happiness', all we should have for the fellow man is compassion. No judgement is needed as we are all the same, we are all having a human experience. Nevertheless, sometimes we can't find the answers, empathy or support from ourselves alone, and that is more than ok.

In this practice of Love Light Work we will be asking a friend, family member or work colleague to assist our self-development in our emotional progression. You need to ask someone you are close to for a list of kind words that they associate with you, in return for some kind words you associate with them.

When you have received the word offerings, it is time to start writing your positive affirmations. A positive affirmation is a sentence that you read out loud in front of the mirror, so you can see and hear for yourself a kind truth that the brain will register.

In time you can add more positive or future manifestations of your own, yet it is helpful to start with a loved one's words, as you know these are one hundred percent true.

For example,

I AM AN INSPIRING SPIRIT

or

I AM A KIND PERSON

Do this every morning for 90 days to begin with and see how different your reality becomes when you are surrounded with words of love.

Element Thirteen

Alignment.

"With the right alignment, everything you want makes its way into your experience, you are the keeper of your own gate"

Abraham Hicks

Love Will Always Find a Way

Love will always find a way.
Even when you feel abandoned,
the ability to let go of a love that doesn't serve you
will make the room.

When the Universe removes a love you were willing to change for,
the plan could never be swayed.

As when we say goodbye to that which is no longer meant to be experienced,
we are blessed with an abundance of love without judgement.

So, leave the loves that don't set your heart on fire,
leave your mind stimulated and your soul searching,
because today you've received the magic of you through time.

An Eternal Truth

To let the words slip out unfettered
is a message so old that it creates a space of eternal truth.

For the words were made in magic with a future of laughter,
while you were getting lost in you,
this was the only map to truly finding yourself.

To feel the most complete in a moment of nothing
creates so much warmth in our souls,
that it feels like you can shine so hard
that you transmute through space and time.

As the minutes move by,
a soul finally finishes a story,
with words filled with so much love
that they spill into the stories of others.

Magic in Minutes

I've never felt more me than with you.
The only version of love that you can truly feel
is the one that has been left untold.

To love in the moments that feel wasted,
yet nevertheless manifest so much abundance,
is not to be judged.

As magic meets in minutes,
we don't think into it
and just accept the gifts of a unique time and bond.

A clear connection of consciousness and passion,
a movement of poetry that only the two can share,
as it's their world now and anything can happen.

With trust and a sweet sincerity,
they soar into the skies like a shooting star of trust.

Free Your Voice

When the words you speak aren't thought about
a conversation of the soul can be created.

To enter the element of magic has no method
this can only come from Source,
an ever-magical connection of trust.

To realise that we are one with the music and the lyrics
is the real gift of life.
Letting go of the material will only manifest.

So, keep flowing with every word,
don't overthink baby that's not the way to go,
just feel the moment and free your voice.

We Are Meant to Change

Just like it takes two wings to create the flight of a butterfly,
remember the love will only keep flying when it is at ease.

The flutter of a partnership of self
is sent to create a love beat that spreads a metamorphosis of soul.

The cocoon of isolation and self-love happens on the inside
and without anyone noticing the miracle of change.

The enchantment can't be understood by the outside world,
nevertheless, a beauty grows and transforms into a new reality
that will eventually be seen by the eye of man.

Just remember dear spirit,
we are meant to change.
Even if this takes time,
you will always create your divine.

The Light Hits You

Remember who you are now,
the girl with so much love that it's the only language you can understand.

The shadows will always be there
but can only be seen in the light.
The dark past that says you aren't enough
is the transparent trap that is the past.

So, keep that shadow at your side
don't let it escape
and settle yourself into the physical form you have become.

The one that has spirit so pure,
has all the dreams made inside.
So, don't go off the deep end.
The fear is only there because you are scared of what you may lose.

The loss isn't here, live in the moment, move in your own way
and love the ones that only love you,
allow the others to rest in a confusion of self-pity.

The Beginning of the End

When the beginning is the end to the beginning of the end
only then can you release into how it's meant to feel.

Love on all levels through the intimacy of the loyal two,
their paths crossed too many times for them not to travel together.

The world is their home as they are free hearts that take a vow to each other
to create the beautiful bounty of what will be.

So, sleep dear past.
You will be treasured and treated with respect,
the sincere sacrifice is the only thing we can align with.

So, move into the new world of love of the authentic
with soul, passion and the divine.
This is our time.

Knowing that Time

In the past, having to run away to be yourself was the only secret I knew,
yet this running made me fall into you.

Living each other's lives for another
is a story that only the woke understand.

The perfect alignment of knowing the time, DNA and rules,
is only a tale that mankind has told to steal our soul's destinations.

So, it's time to play with our own paragraphs
of how we want to pass,
as it is only in the end when we find our peace with truth.

Escaping into You

Escaping into you, escaping into me.
Moving into new galaxies of stardust and magic,
the lovers with no limits.

The fantasy begins with a journey of integrity
And a sincere trust in the eternal flame of lust's love fire.

As they chart out the course they want to travel,
stars shine to help them find the way.

So, whenever each feels lost,
all they have to do is look up at the astronomical maps they have created
to feel at home in each other's unique Universe.

Solace in Connection

Apart yet still together in their solace,
always in connection.
Hearts that are now flames; the smoke has dissipated.

The cracks filled with sunshine and souls,
vow that it won't ever be like it was,
each other's treasure of expression.

The gold seal that burns a beat of solid love,
peace and purity.
With practice the lovers grow.

The heat of the heart keeps growing
as it heals the burnt cells of pity
beginning in their pure domain.

Alignment Meditation

The Alignment Light work practice is one that aims to align you with the Earth beneath your feet, and the great, expansive Universe above your head. It is an awareness of how small we are compared to the great encompassing realm we inhabit. The Alignment meditation is one of a circular visual breathwork meditation that aligns you to receive the energies of the Mother Earth and the Grandfather Universe.

To begin, find a calm place where you won't get disturbed. Sit upright on a chair with your palms on your lap facing up, your head up straight and your feet planted on the floor bare footed. This is so you will receive the energy of the earth through your feet and the universal prana energy through your head (crown chakra) and your palms; these are your very own charging stations.

Now as you sit, I want you to connect. Close your eyes and breath. Now think of the Earth, the idea of its layers and the core of Earth that gives so much of its power to all of its plains and inhabitants. The colour you are going to connect with and draw from is gold; this will be drawn through your body as you inhale. When you exhale, visualise the gold core energy flowing through your vessel and being released into the Universe. Repeat this full breath cycle for 10 full breaths.

Now it's time to receive from the above. So now with your breathing, inhale and connect to the universal white pure light energy, receive it and breathe this into the Earth. Visualise the white light energising and cleansing your body as it channels the energy through the layers of life-giving soil. Repeat this cycle for 10 full breaths. If you are enjoying this meditation and wish to expand it, add more breath cycles.

The alignment to the Sources helps us to align with the reality of self and how lucky we are to be a part of this process of life. We are the catalysts of the Earth and Universe, our vessels take in healing energies and become revitalised, as we are part of the process which connects Grandmother Earth to Grandfather Ether.

Element Fourteen

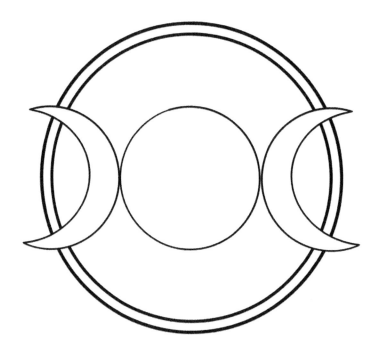

Power.

"We become what we think about. Energy flows where attention goes."

Rhonda Byrne.

The Battle of the Phoenix

Though she had only stepped a little over the edge,
the fear was overwhelming.
Others thought she was brave
and this was the push she needed.

The woman she was about to become
would set the path behind her on fire,
in the unravelling of traumatic release,
the phoenix arises.

The battle will keep on coming,
but this warrior goddess will only find a new skill to bring to the fight,
as the power of her will is never-ending.

For she does not duel for her,
it's for the army,
the ones she teaches the skills to,
as they are the ones who will stand up, in time.

The ones that will be able to do battle
when the day turns to dark,
to brighten up the black with their sparks of pure power.

For this strength has been made over the decades
and is now moving from the body and mind,
to the spirit.

This energy is everlasting,
we experience few movements in the physical form,
so, sharpen your sword of spirit
and soar into your endless bright.

The Fragile Forest

Turn your pain into your lessons
and help the ones that are still a few steps behind,
as you are breaking through the trees that scrape the skin
and venturing out into the plains of peace.

The dark may seem real
as the layers of sadness engulf the embrace of your release.
Remember, though the forest is strong the branches can grow fragile.

One by one, snap through the tundra of time
because now is the escape
into the life you were once held captive from,
your canopy of crystals.

For the fall of envy became their poison, not yours,
an apple plucked from the branch,
yet the kiss that reawakens has to happen in this time.

A kiss of love,
support and tenderness.
Wipe away the years that were stolen away from your glorious soul
and become the princess
the beast was keeping for himself.

The beauty is always hidden for a reason,
for the right time for you to become the one who can lead others.
It's you,
the priestess of light.

Rest in Peace Princess

As the anger rises from every cell,
access it in the other realm,
for the passion can be driven
into the power of self.

Rip in two to rest in peace
and start the seance of the spell
that casts who one will always be.

The princess has now left the castle,
but the queen will remain.
With all her loves lost,
her fierce force will be felt from miles away,
her voice the casting of magic.

Her energy is a field of true magnetism,
of intense female power.

Her kingdom is on its knees in suppliance,
eager to sip from her chalice of charisma
and engage with the inner charge
that released the girl
and recruited the warrior woman.

They will rise together
because in unity we are one,
strong femininity –
anything can be done.

Petal by Petal

Little lotus, listen to the contrast,
the feeling of unease,
it isn't worth going back to.
I know it can't be done without release.

It is time to explore,
create and become so proud,
that you bloom into brilliance,
to shine be proud.

Be the spirit you desire to be,
because little lotus today is the present
and it is time to unfold leaf by leaf,
petal by petal until you get to the gift.

The gift of being you,
every element of you so unique,
all my love little lotus I've given you.

Notice the Break

Take care dear spirit,
take care in what words you think.

It takes time to heal and speak,
some days are so full you don't notice the breakout,
please allow the heart to feel.

Those little lines that were once broken
are coming back in gold thread notes of love's sonnet,
ready to come and be remembered.

The love does not have to come from another one,
take care dear spirit with the words you speak,
bring in the love from way down deep.

She is listening with clear pages,
So, speak the truth of love well said.

Don't Turn Out the Light

Your love and respect are all that you have,
so, treat others as you would like to be treated.

No regrets,
just take the time and really see,
there's a lot in this world
that needs to be.

Strength,
courage,
truth and honesty.
The way we live is the way we are completed.

Be the one that fights for the right,
do not be defeated,
do not turn out the light
and be cheated.

Love yourself compassionately,
give thanks for all you have,
because dear spirit,
the battle has just begun.
Let that love flow through your field and make the difference,
be transmitted for that reason.
Everyone is waiting to wake up.

She is Water

Like the water,
she is ever changing.
Through the troubled current she held on,
with the knowledge that she had the power to change it all.

Her tide has pulled back,
and released the sands of self-love,
that sparkle with pride and power.

For she may seem calm
but whilst the ripples rest,
their eb and flow can destress.

For she is the power of the mother,
and she will crash into the rocks if she needs to.

Don't underestimate her intensity for her kin,
for she is water
and her power is to change.

Passion for the People

I am here to hold your hand,
and rest assured the vow is yours.
Past promises of pride
you have paid with peace.

For all who allow and let go
the true self will be your love,
love of life,
love of self,
love of others,
as we are one.

The one that creates this world,
the ones who help this world,
the ones who set their souls free.

Passion for the people is the only plan,
creating a better Earth is the only vision.

So sweet spirit,
just keep driving for the lives you are about to change,
make this your decision,
to keep on your mission.

Pinning of Peace

Pinning my peace on you,
Was only wasted time,
the protection you misread for passion misled.

For the pressure was pain,
and the creation of the festered divine
was a message of sincere distress
of all past emotions.

The tales that couldn't release for you weren't the guide
but the mentor of madness.
Distraction is always your true mate.

She slept in your sorcery for too long and now awakens,
for only her Source knows best.

The lesson of not listening to the world,
will never be replayed.
For she only talks in truth,
and time will bring ink to the page.
Laced in Every Cell
For when she awakes,
that is when her dreams begin;
this girl with magic laced in every cell.

She has slept for many years
to appease and succumb
which made the others win,
still her soul is in magnificent release.

Her tribe connects with good intent, for as she shines,
others wish for passion,
power,
and the purpose of the thrill.

So, don't go back to the rest,
be a testament to your best,
as this is how the ether works -
you traded times of sincere will.

Trust me sister, now is now
and magic happens when we trust.
Wake from the past hate of gone days,
to align with your love in so many ways.

Manifestation Meditation

This power is in your mind. All your heart's desires are attainable, yet you have to know what these desires are before you can bring them into your life.

A Manifestation Meditation is a visual meditation, these can take a while to progress with, a good practice technique is guided meditation, as they can ignite the mind's power.

Before the meditation, think and write down what you would like to bring into your life - be specific!

If you need an aid, look online to find pictures of what you wish to manifest, you could even make a vision board to look at pre-visualisation meditation. A vision board is several images of what you want to bring into your life, stuck to a piece of paper or framed. Have this somewhere you can see it, so you can become aware of the visuals you are attracting.

Before the meditation, watch your visual aid for at least one minute before you begin.

Make sure you are in a comfortable position: either sat upright in a chair with your feet flat on the floor or cross-legged, the spine should be aligned and neutral at all times, or you can lie on the floor in a Shavasana position. Then slowly close your eyes, relax your shoulders, loosen your brow and soften your jaw.

To begin with, we are going to balance your breathing and release the body, so inhale a deep breath and hold, as you do this, tighten all of your body and hold it. While you exhale, release and then repeat this technique 4 times.

Now flow into an organic breathing rhythm. Your body and mind are now clear to start the manifestation process, so envision your dreams - be it a healthier body, more friends, a beautiful new home, or a holiday. The secret is to create a memory, feel the moment and see the happiness that is connected for you in those visuals.

Go for 5-30 minutes and make sure you are in a space in which you won't be disturbed. This forecasting method of meditation is a powerful tool to align with what you want to work towards in your life.

After the practice, draw on how the manifestation process you created in your practice made you feel. You can add things or take them away, be aware when you have brought something into your life and when you do, celebrate it. This meditation can bring about great changes if you let it, and if you are diligent enough to practice this behaviour often, the results will overflow into all areas of your life, in time.

Have trust in your power and for all that is around you, supporting your life with love and light.

Happy dream making!

Element Fifteen

Awakening.

"To realise you are not your thoughts is when you begin to awaken spiritually"

Eckhart Tolle

Colours Without Control

Sometimes you've got to love the wrong people
for the right ones to be found and cared for.

When you feel lost in the endeavour of an endless unrequited love
you slowly start to break
and when the heart is finally opened
it can find someone true.

To hold on even when they aren't around
as they will always have a piece of your soul to flourish with.

A connection that is on a conscious level of all existence
and is as wild as the flowers that give colour without control.

Dance of Sweet Mystery

In love with an eternal world that you thought no one would get.
An entanglement of moments that make no sense to the human,
only to the soul.

To live in a movement of wonder sets the heart free
to seek a new way of life.
To give everything is the only awakening

To truly have opened your third eye
is to see the mysteries and manifestations of the world
that make perfect resonance.

As creation is made from within
and this is when we can only truly begin
to live to flow into your next dance.

Caretakers of Healing

To be able to handle the darkest secret that you have kept,
was the key that unlocked the door to a new space of time.

For minutes are manmade,
like the ideals of a society which has been fed on greed,
that lose the ability to talk in emotion.

Holdback the words that could really release
the constrictions of a make-believe constitution,
that holds the energetic in the cell of a society born dying.

To really feel is only a gift a few of the caretakers of healing can experience.
Yet this ability needs to heal itself first
before we can be set free to wake up the loved ones
we want to share our lives with.

Us to Us

From us to us,
it's time to wake up and tear away at man's past way of thinking.
What were you thinking?

How you feel is a way into the soul
in which you can easily feel lost
with what has been taught by fear
to cage your creativity.

Life doesn't have to be black and white all the time,
ask yourself who has really made these rules.
When we realise that the golden tickets to what we desire
are no longer for the few,
the magic will start to appear.

We are all divine and made into our own time
with the second birthing of what we call the life lessons.

Cutting away at the unconscious cord,
is the process you must act on
or you will start to disappear.

Worlds in Worlds

The worlds in worlds,
the never-ending shifts of egos
and a release for when we feel the unease of honesty.
It can all go amiss.

Nevertheless, for love it sometimes isn't time,
you have to travel through the locations of layered anguish
to find the portal of soul connection.

For you can only find what you seek from within
to know what your life journey will ask.
Sometimes we don't trust the path that has been walked on.

We try to find shortcuts to the life we so desire,
yet when we stop and look around
we are living our path of integrity.

So, stop travelling to miss what is yours
and trust in the magic that's at your door.
For it will come knocking,
just wait and see.
The love that makes your heart complete.
You.

Riddle of Society

When your eyes truly open,
it can hurt the soul more than the first sight at birth,
when we have only experienced purity.

As the years pass it possesses the spirit with a riddle of society,
of the ways we have been made to conform
to only exist and not live.

Taking a slice of the authentic you,
in each segment of time that the reality has blindfolded you with
can first taste foreign,
with each bite you seek a familiar truth.

For when you awake
you will see that the only thing that is real is the way you feel,
the internal spilling over into the world that created your fake core beliefs.

When the melancholy mix of emotion, vibration and truth
becomes the frequency that you make your home in the universe,
will it only then open the gates.

Soul's Palm

No time for us because there is no time for you,
run away from the love that was the only freedom of your soul.

The race won't take it away,
the past is gone
nevertheless, it happened dear one.
Holding onto this life so hard will only cause pain.

As when we hold onto anything too hard it crushes.
So sweet one, treat this life like a flower left to grow,
let it have sunshine,
talk to it with care
and don't pick it to crush it in your soul's palm.

Don't forget who we saw.
A Source full of manifestation and angelic connection.
The beast can slumber, you can awake now dear child.

The nightmares have gone,
you have experienced pure love, pure acceptance, and pure authenticity.
All you have to do,
is pour that into you.

So, take this time to rest to wake.
No more dismay, for its your time to walk with your best friend, you.

Sit with Yourself

Time for you isn't so easy as it sounds,
for when you don't want to sit with yourself,
how can another?

To distract and try to dull the stolen voice of your heart's pain,
can only cause dis-ease
and in time only scare you further.

The escape of not wanting to feel has become your life's masterpiece.
Yet even in seclusion your lessons are not free to teach.

For the wise one you think you are,
is only hiding the heart's art of unmeasurable love.

Be your own world,
because that is more connected than stepping into the real one.

Pieces of a Poet

Picking up the pieces of a poet that came to the point of pain,
that processed a change that let go of her life.

The changed script of a soul that couldn't hear the voice of Source anymore
had to pass over to another.

As to keep on in so much torture tore this writer apart
into a shadow of self.

Losing everything, only to gain access to another realm,
where a connection to self and others was made in pure love.

So sometimes you have to break to become whole,
a secret that society stole away from you.

Paint the stars of the authentic self
to mix in the melody of the universe
that has always been waiting to live with you.

Split to Begin

Time to break.
This is the only way you can become you,
like the seed of what life's manifestation will be.
First, we have to split to begin.

Break until the next process can start,
then you can enter your endless involvement in love's story.

For when we start living in the stages of struggle
we work into our own unique beauty.

The growth will be different for all living,
from the simple daisy to the grand oak,
each journey is as important as each other's.

So, push through each layer of dirt,
that will be your test,
to live your life's rich story of being the best.

Awakening exercise

Statements and views surrounding body type, lifestyle choices or what we should wear are often controlled, maintained and profited off. If we believe these views it can create a core belief in us that can manipulate our relationship with self. These tailored doctrines are designed to cause us unease, and we can create unhealthy mind maps about ourselves which can affect our lives and how we think in a damaging way. This can cause the creation of opinions about one's self that are unkind, and words or behaviour that we would never say or behave like to others.

The Awakening exercise is made to shake you up out of commercial control and awaken you to a connection to self which operates from love. This won't be the easiest of light work practices in this book, yet when we are aware of the mind's mantras of unhelpful behaviours, we can start the work to awaken to the beautiful reality of how magical we really are. To be in your simplest form, to be able to take in this incredible journey of life, is a gift many won't experience. It is a miracle that we were even born and experience life. Be grateful for it!

So, to begin with we are going to get ourselves in a space where nobody can disturb us. We need this peace so we can fully attune to our inner critique, the little voice that's trying to keep you safe yet has been moulded by capitalist intention.

You will need a pen and paper. Now it's time to get honest with yourself, this isn't going to be a pleasant experience, but you must write down all the things you don't like about yourself, think you're not capable of, every little bit of nasty nonsense you have formed with the opinions of others. Get these out of your mind and onto that paper, issues with body type, behaviour, lifestyle choices etc. Now look at that hard and think about placing all that bullying onto someone else. Pretty mean right?

That wasn't very nice was it? So why do we have that relationship with self, yet not with others? Let's get it clear, let's get rid of that palaver that's taking space in your creative, unique, gifted brain.

So, after you have spilled all that nonsense onto the page, get ready to say goodbye to that piece paper.

You can rip it up, or if you have a safe way of burning it, do so. Say it out loud 'I DONT NEED YOU ANYMORE!'.

Let it all go, it's time to start again and awaken to a reality which is waiting for you with gratitude, peace and love, because everyone deserves happiness.

To calm down after, why not try the Connection meditation?
This will rebalance you after an emotional Light Work.
I hope you feel freer.

Element Sixteen

Divinity.

"Every man is a divinity in disguise,
a god playing the fool"

Ralph Waldo Emerson

Edge of Discovery

To completely find yourself takes a journey to the edge of discovery.
As we create distance from a society of man,
we can learn to identify who we really are.

The escape of a soul that's voice needed to be nurtured by silence
becomes a sweet symphony of sincerity.

The notes that sometimes bring a message
that molded a magic moment of music and mystery
can only be solved with the connection to Source.

The rivers of trust,
the lands of old,
and sands of time,
that tether the solitary soul
and grant you control.
A lost child wants to be found inside.

The Universe is Within Me

I want you to come find yourself with me.
Dive into a deep mystery of love and enchantment.

For the Universe is within me so come star,
seek some soul secrets
to make us shoot into the galaxies of greatness.

So, keep searching to complete the astrology of our lovers' quest,
as when the Earth and ether meet
the discovery is found.

Locating where the grey matter can manifest
to create what was always meant to be,
the twin flames take off in cosmic pleasure.

Ocean's Souls

Why ache, my dear heart?
Your love has not gone,
they are just waiting for the tide to come in again,
for the moment when you can retouch.

This is like the sun,
setting on the seas that touch the waters
to drape the magic of stardust into the deep.

That divine moment that nurtures all life,
within the emotional waves of femininity,
and trusts with the sparkle of life.

The touch of sincerity that rides on the ocean's soul
to stop the heart from longing for the solar shine.

Help the Embers Heal

To have been lost in lives of anxiety
was a message the body always was trying to get through to you,
as you have a sense that not many are blessed with.

To have been admired,
yet with no recognition of the awe
was a different lesson for the flames of love.

As the two fire souls walked side by side
in a coincidence of collective of healing,
they taught the truth of the story they started to kindle.

All it would take is the time we have created in our minds
to help the emotional embers burn.
As when we realise that every second is perfect,
we can heal the Earth of us.

Love from an Angel

To trust every word and for it to feel so easy,
was a new space in her spirit.
The light was the healer through the medicine that molded.

For the energy was regifted in so many ways,
a touch of the body,
a song of the heart,
and words of the mind.

The gifts that don't cost anything are the priceless ones
and every moment of the present awoke the lovers' scroll.

To rest in the knowledge that her love could not be sold,
yet with love from an angel,
the world could behold the gifts of pleasure,
a kiss from a soul.

A Flame Breaks in Two

To be kept at the gates to nowhere
was the everlasting struggle of a soul
that was already enchanted within another.

For when a flame breaks in two,
it will burn with a fear of loneliness
that only the other half will ever feel.

To be with others and still miss you
was the forever heartbreak of a life of torment
that cracked the human into an angel.

As when the flames were at the last level of their fairytale,
they finally intwined to create a manifestation of an infinite love.

Scars of a Heart

You left scars on a heart that broke and shattered through the Universe
so, it could be scattered and safe.
This was the quest of a soul learning to let go.

One love of two lives that are only whole when together,
living in another reality of a pure love
that's energy has always been manifesting.

The paths of the star-crossed lovers,
passing by one whilst the other felt the absence of a flame,
a mate,
a love,
that would ease the ache of a heart's space.

The patience has created a space filled with endless creation,
as this present of conscious connection
creates a life of miracles.

A Feather in the Wind

To sit back and realise you are allowed to feel again has set love free,
like the most beautiful hummingbird in flight.

Even though they are rare to see,
beholding their beauty is so intense
that it imprints on the mind
and will remain there all of time.

Through the window of the divine
we have the pleasure of capturing the beauty of a creature so shy
yet magnificent.
Now to begin the story of setting it free.

For when we allow the flight and flow,
we become like a feather in the wind: unaware of time.
This is where the enchantment begins,
through the beauty and divine.

Angel Lost

I know it's hard to stay baby.
I know it's hard to live in a world that wasn't meant for you.
You have always been an angel lost.

Time is the healer, even though it is our test.
So please wrap your wings around yourself
because we find it so hard not to miss you dear angel.

Even though we see your smile in the sparkles of sunset,
your laughter in the breeze,
and your touch on the raindrops that cleanse our souls.

There's no forgiveness needed sweet star child;
you were too big for this world.
So, create your magic in the Universe
and we will be sure to look up at the stars to see you shine.

A Promise to the Stars and Back

I know that from a space of pain and hostility I can still grow,
as you are my sunshine,
one of the ones that helped me know.

With an unconditional love that kept me on this land
when all my spirit wanted was to break free,
the tether could have only been your innocent command.

The angels were heaven sent to test us.
I understand that it's hard,
yet if it were easier,
we would not grow.

I swear to the stars and back,
I will keep my promise to love and protect our dear lives.

Dream to believe
and ask away to create a life so serene.

Divinity Exercise

As we are the most creative, independently thinking, ambitious species on this planet, are we really aware of our connection to the divine?

The divine has many names and forms: God, the Universe, Allah. Nevertheless, whatever manifestation you follow, it is important to understand that we are made in his vision and we are loved beyond compare.
Do we really appreciate how incredible we are?
Do we see our true selves and reach for our dreams with pride and confidence?

The divine light work is one of prayer. This might not be for everyone, yet this practice has changed my relationships with others, myself, food and my habits. So, I believe it should have a place in this book and your everyday lives, if you so choose.

You will need a candle, a lighter and a pleasant environment. This practice is to be done daily to see the gratitude you have for a life that is perfect at all times, that creates growth and awakens you to the gifts that all can receive. All it takes is a minute, it's about consistency and quality not quantity - this is your time to be thankful.

I pray in the morning, usually after making breakfast and preparing the home for the wonderful family that I am blessed to have.
I light my candle, and, in my head, I say thanks.
Thank you, Universe, for the day ahead, for my family being safe and happy, for the ability to love and respect myself. Thank you for the running water, shelter, and food we receive. Thank you, God.

You can add whatever you are thankful for in life. This is the real law of attraction, coming from a high vibrational state of love rather than desperation. Prayers of these kind don't get received like they do when we say our prayers through sweet love.

After your prayer, blow your candle out and make a wish for you or anything that is in your vortex.
You have the ability to change your life with the power of divine prayer.

Element Seventeen

Source.

"When we experience our own desire for transformation, we are feeling the Universe evolving through us"

Barbara Marx Hubbard

Moving the Shifts

When the heart fools you,
don't forget,
that the love for ourselves and our kin is the only truth.

The loss of love's connection,
of play and pleasure,
was once taken for granted
and has ripped the lovers in two.

For the love they had,
she couldn't see,
as the girl was lost
in past tragedy.

She won't mourn every dawn,
she will embrace the support of the energy that surrounds
and allow the teachings the mother has to offer.

Reaching into the pain and fear,
no more pretending,
the shifts are moving
with the knowledge of her ancestors and power past.

Mother You

Mother Nature.
Mother you.
Mother who?

Listen to her soul's demand.
This event is not by chance,
it's time to heal and elevate.

Start singing,
shine to celebrate,
for this is earth,
our heaven sent
and we are the angels here to ascend.

To raise as one and co-create,
to rip away the shades of disgrace,
let's join hands and remember well.

The past,
the present,
this moment now.

Life on the Run

Forget me not,
dear stealer of dreams,
and drive to dare,
for I cannot live my life on the run.

To fear ourselves,
will not bring back yesterday,
don't go back dear sincere soul,
your journey is just about to unfold.

Throw yourself into the world
and design your constellations in cosmic design,
as the reality will fade away.

Wake up,
dive in,
drip into every space of time,
awake the guides of your past energy,
this is not the time to slumber.

The future is coming back,
to sway and sing you into the paradigm
with passion and devotion.

Earth Traveller

Dear Earth traveller,
what is your name?
How did you come to this place?

What is your purpose?
and what is the path?
Do you believe all about your past?

The lives are there,
the futures that have been told,
so just be present and behold.
Revel in love connection and sheer joy.

Dear Earth traveller,
don't be sold,
don't give up on your goals,
just live with those old messages,
close to your soul.

Waiting in the Sky

The friends and foes,
of past and new,
will always see
a new version of you.

Just know your worth
and don't make haste.
Sit with the moments,
see how they taste.

Align with you,
and progress my dear,
as the past will only make you sincere.

So, stop stooping
and look up high,
the messages are waiting
in the sky.

Meant to Change

When you look back,
remember how far you have come,
all your life's experiences,
that you have become.

Yes, song sister, you aren't the same,
as baby you were meant to change.

Be brave,
and speak your word,
carry the message,
as angel girl you are heard.

Words aren't the only form of connection
you know,
energy is real
and it always steals the show.

Open up and feel,
sit in the silence so you can reveal.

Be the greater good,
take away your pride
because this is the only time,
you can really shine.

Different Girl

To the girl that dared to be different,
and let her dreams be real,
the one that lives in magic,
with love that makes the deal.

For she is a sunshine soul,
this goddess girl,
a forever youth,
of endless joy and authenticity.

This dazzling dancer that's moving around the world,
her story must be told,
as her lessons became her strength,
like tales of old.

To be an inspiration to all she meets,
keep on pirouetting princess through this space,
in time it's divine.

Release into Reality

This is your last night,
The last night to pretend,
the last night of the lies,
the last night of the obstacles.

For the next time darkness falls,
you will release into the reality
of the Universe inside you.

For beauty was made in tragedy,
where the slow drip of the unsure lived tethered,
and withered the soul for too long.

Trust in the mother
and the mother you are.
Remember,
you are worthy of love and you are loved.

So, live in every cell that has the messages of your past,
to be unique is enchanting
and you don't have to hide.

No more pity for the other side,
for they will never understand,
and this is the way.
For if we all aligned the truth,
it couldn't be discovered.

So, shine dear star seed,
your story is one of other worlds,
just be you,
just be who you are.

The Glitter that Lived Within the Child

With all the beauty you can't see,
let others be the eyes to your experience.
The glitter that lived within the child will sparkle when you listen.

Allow the levitation of love and vibrant connection,
as you don't have to be scared anymore,
the beasts of unsure now live within their cages.

The angels now stand guard,
only allow the purity and passion
of the highest form of love abundance that is heaven sent.

The prayers and praise you have been so privileged to forecast
are the magic that the manifestation needed.

Beautiful and brave,
step out into the clouds,
as the mist has cleared
and the sun is everlasting
and shining through.

So, live with a smile brave soul, the lessons you have learnt,
have created this pure ultimate bliss.

The Fire's Tale

That last part of pain
that hangs on to show you it was real, a breath that won't go as deep,
to say goodbye makes it real.

To move on is to release that last memory,
of walking on the beach at sunset
and knowing it was the last day.

To lie under the stars,
while you watch the fire,
tells its own tale –
that the magic was never meant to last.

Each pang of love you let go,
teaches you why you lived in such vigour.
With every step, memory and lie
you had to say goodbye.

Be brave little soul,
it's time to let go,
I know it's hard,
nevertheless, it's time,
to spread your wings
and fly up high.

A Walk in Nature Practice

To connect with the divine of you, there is only one way that a purer consciousness can be channelled - this is not through ego.
Even though Source is internal, it is the magic from the earth, the Universes and the other divine beings that walk this path with you. Source is pure love, connection to consciousness, the universal laws of being.

So how do we align with the love that wraps us up in every moment, dimension and choice of our human experience?

Well this is one of the most stunning gifts that all of us on planet Earth have been blessed with, Mother Earth herself:

Nature.

Nature is an offering of Source, a deep connection to your truth and the messages that will comfort, enlighten and awaken, in order to assist with the transition into our new energetic planet.

This Light Work exercise soothes and enlightens in a perfect synchronicity that will help access your higher self and Source.

A walk in nature can be so restorative and ensures that you are taking in the medicines that Mother Nature intended to nurture your cells with.
This Light Work practice can be adapted to any of the plains on the planet: beaches, forests, mountains, fields, or any garden that Gaia supports.

To begin with, make sure you have no distractions like a phone for example. A journal and pen are great tools to add more value to the practice, so even in the times you can't receive nature's tonic, you can reflect on the pages for solace and love.

Before stepping into your natural landscape, feel it. Stand still or sit down, feel the breeze softly caress your skin, the sun charging your cells, the rain cleansing your soul or the gales blowing away the cobwebs. No weather is bad weather, Source has sent this elemental to do its energetic work for your higher good.

Once you're grounded with the feeling, attune your sense of smell, gently feel the cold air you are inhaling and the warm air your vessel is providing in return. Take in the sweet woodland, its spring fragrances, or the crisp, musk tones of autumn. When you are near the seas, take in the salt to balance. In the mountains, inhale the pines that have unique reviving properties in order to awaken your sacred life visions.

Organically, by moving into the third element of grounding, your vision will start speaking to you as you start to notice how the landscape you are in is supporting the wildlife. The wildlife that puts trust in us that all will be provided, see the fruitful trees, the seas that support the aquatic domain or the heathers on the mountain tops, that have the insect kingdom's best interest at heart. Nature is working together in balance, trust that this is what we must feel to our cores, the love and support for this is one of the only real truths.

A few examples of questions you can ask yourself after the grounding process are:

How are the elements/weather making me feel today?

What season is coming next and what will that bring?

How has that tree managed to grow to the strong structure before you?

What smells can I take in?

How does the acorn grow into the oak?

What are the patterns on the trees?

What colours are the flowers and leaves?

What animals can you see?

What is the ground like?

Why do you like being here?

What do you feel like here?

If near water:

What is the water's mood?

Does the water change?

How does the water benefit us and the ecosystem?

Are all grains of sand the same?

Feel. Be present and remember nature is always with you. Reflect on your answers and try to expand the questions to connect with your own divine truth.

You are loved, you are beautiful, you are as unique as each snowflake; never the same but beautiful in their own essence

Love and Light.

I hope you enjoy your Source Light Work practice in Nature.

Connect to the truth of you with the support of Source of mother earth.

ACKNOWLEDGEMENTS & APPRECIATIONS

Firstly, I would like to thank my sons for being my anchor to life and the reason I get up and try to excel every day in being a role model as a solo parent, and to show you that anything is possible on this plain called Earth.

To my parents, Julie & Trevor. I know I can be hard to understand, yet you still love me regardless and support me on all levels of life. For this I thank you.

Next is my family of soul sisters, my tribe of beautiful women. I am so grateful and humbled to have such a tribe of creative, tenacious, spiritual, badass babes by my side. Booyaah ladies!

To my twin flame, Ste. Thank you for collaborating on the illustrations and book cover for Lotus Lifting. I am so thankful for your sterling advice, honest love and support. Thank you, I love you.

Time to get deep now and give some mega big up love to Abraham-Hicks. Gosh, I don't know if I would be here without you. THANK YOU!

Thank you to the medicine of the Amazon rainforest for making me well in body, mind and soul.

Thank you to Tanja & Lars Faber and collective, for my first ceremony of release in holotropic breath work at the Sacred Temple in Zinfandel Holland.

Thank you to Peru, for bringing the information of Ayahausca to me and aligning me with my Intercessor, Shaura Hall, who I was lucky enough to access the healing of the mother with through the medicine. This allowed me to access love and take steps towards my higher self.

Thank you to John Wilson, for helping me on my spiritual path with third eye kambo awakening, you are such a special man in the community.

A big thank you to Paul Boys, the Reiki Master who helped clear past lives that were suppressing my connection to the Ether and who helped me access my divine connection to access the gifts of light work to shine onto others.

Thank you to the full power Liam Browne, the magic man who helped open my heart with his gift and ceremony of precious Cacao, your energetic laugh and supportive soul is such a gift to the ones blessed to have shared the same space as you.

Thank you to my Reiki master and Earth angel: Andrea Nyland, who is my teacher of the spiritual realm. I owe my future connection to Source and ongoing developments to her works.

I thank the courses in holistic, Reiki, life-coaching, mindfulness and meditation that helped me form these practices.

For the quotes used, I thank Abraham Hicks, Eckhart Tolle, Deepak Chopra, Dalai Lama, Louise Hay, Wayne Dwyer, Mahatama Gandhi, Rhonda Byrne, Babara Marx Hubbard, Rumi. Your books and quotes have inspired me to pass them onto others, so that you can reach their souls and help them like you did mine, thank you.

Thank you to my editor Jarvis Carr, your constant work and commitment to communication made the entire process that much easier.

Last but not least thank you, you beautiful, beautiful readers. I hope the channelled poetry from Source, the quotes of my spiritual teachers and the Light Work practices have helped you access self-love, acceptance and an abundance of joy in your wonderful human experience. Serving others is my passion and to wake the world up to their unique, beautiful power and potential is the path that has chosen me.

LOVE LIGHT & ALIGNMENT.

All the best bits,
Clairine
xoxo

Printed in Great Britain
by Amazon

82396285R00147